Obentoo 2
Workbook

べんとう

Anne Fisher   Ayako Fukunaga

Kyoko Kusumoto   Jean Swinyard

THOMSON

NELSON

Australia · Canada · Mexico · Singapore · Spain · United Kingdom · United States

THOMSON

NELSON

102 Dodds Street
Southbank Victoria 3006

Email nelson@thomsonlearning.com.au
Website http://www.thomsonlearning.com.au

First published in 1999
10 9 8 7 6 5
05 04 03 02

Copyright © 1999 Nelson Australia Pty Limited.

Designed by Judith Summerfeldt-Grace, Jacinta Hanrahan, Mary Baldwin
Cover illustration by Bronek Kózka
Illustrations by Kae Sato-Goodsell
Cover designed by Judith Summerfeldt-Grace
Editor Catriona McKenzie
Project editor Ingrid De Baets
Publishing Editor Sally Happell
Typeset in Bembo
Printed in China by L. Rex Printing Co., Ltd

This title is published under tne imprint of Nelson School.
Nelson Australia Pty Limited ACN 058 280 149
(incorporated in Victoria) trading as Nelson Thomson Learning.

Contents

Introduction

Welcome to your *Obentoo 2 Workbook!* The activities in this book will help you practise what you learn in your *Obentoo 2 Student Book.* The tasks in this Workbook are arranged into eight units, corresponding with the eight units in the Student Book, plus かきかた (kanji practice). The content of this book assumes that you are familiar with the vocabulary, patterns and characters introduced in *Obentoo 1.* As you work through this book, you will come across the symbols: 🔲 which shows the content of the task progresses in level of difficulty, 🕊 which refers to a BLM and ちゅうい, who you met in the Student Book, reappears with handy hints. As in *Obentoo 1,* each unit contains a variety of tasks:

- the **listening tasks** 🔊 📱 will develop your understanding of the new language in each unit. Read the instructions for each task carefully and remember to target your listening for the information you need. The sound of the *bell* indicates to pause the recording. If you don't understand everything you hear, don't worry, have a guess; this is what you do in a conversation with a Japanese speaker! If you're having difficulties, think of ways to improve your listening skills: ask your teacher if you can borrow a copy of the CD.

- the **speaking tasks** 🗣🗣 are designed to improve your communicative skills and confidence, so have a go! Speaking is always tricky: you have to think about what you want to say, how to say it, what the other speaker says and whether you have been able to convey your thoughts in a culturally appropriate way! Also remember for creative tasks, such as making up a dialogue, everyone has different ways of organising his/her ideas.

- the **reading tasks** reinforce your understanding of hiragana, katakana and introduce the kanji in realistic contexts. As kanji represent whole 'ideas', you'll find that kanji help you to understand the meaning of sentences quickly. To do this, you will need to learn them well enough to recognise them straight away! The reading tasks will also show you different ways of using the new language - you can use them as models for writing and speaking. Again, remember that you won't always understand everything you read, but if you know what you're looking for, you will pick out what you need!

- the **writing tasks** will help you to practise the new grammar in written sentences and passages. A helpful hint before you start writing, is to brainstorm your ideas (remembering to focus your ideas on what you can say in Japanese) and then write a brief plan. Don't write out everything you want to say in your first language, before you start writing in Japanese! This can be really frustrating, and instead of making you focus on what you *can* say, it only makes you think of things you *want* to say (but maybe can't)!

When you write, think about the writing rules, accuracy of your script and the content. An easy way to check to see what you've written makes sense, is to try to read it back and to translate it into your first language. If it doesn't make sense to you, it probably doesn't in Japanese either!

There is an おべんとう　クイズ at the end of each unit to revise the main content and to help you study for tests. You should try to complete it without referring to your Student Book. If you can't answer every section, note the areas and revise. Your teacher may be able to give you extra work or you may be able to make up some extra practice exercises of your own.

In the かきかた section, you will find kanji writing and reading practice and a fun task for each set of new kanji in the unit.

At the back of this book, there are unit-by-unit Japanese-English word lists with space for you to write in extra words.

ききましょう！はなしましょう！
よみましょう！かきましょう！
がんばってね！

Anne Fisher, Ayako Fukunaga, Kyoko Kusumoto and Jean Swinyard

ゆきさんの　カラオケパーティー

1

Listen to the recording to fill in the time on each clock.

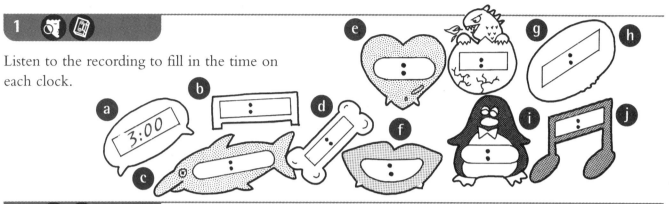

2

Listen to the conversations and fill in the time on each clock. Include *am* or *pm* as appropriate.

3

Circle one of the clock faces you filled in from Task 1. Ask your classmates 「なんじですか」 or answer appropriately, to find someone who has chosen the same time as you.

4

Complete the clock faces below and be sure you know how to say the times in Japanese. Ask five of your classmates 「なんじですか」 and record their initials and score on the scorecard. Don't forget to praise your classmates' efforts by saying すごいですね!

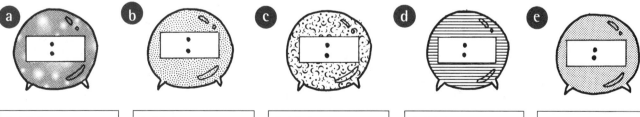

| Initials:_____ | Initials:_____ | Initials:_____ | Initials:_____ | Initials:_____ |
| Score: _____ /5 | Score: _____ /5 | Score: _____ /5 | Score: _____ /5 | Score: _____ /5 |

5

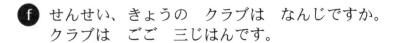

In pairs, read the dialogues and then fill in the times on the clocks. Where appropriate, include *am* or *pm*.

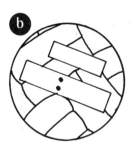

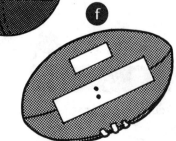

a なんじですか。
ごご　三じです。

b すみません、いま　なんじですか。
いま、ごぜん　十一じです。

c さなえさん、いま　なんじですか。
いま、ごご　四じですよ。

d パーティーは　なんじですか。
パーティーは　ごご　七じです。

e おひる休みは　なんじですか。
おひる休みは　十二じはんです。

f せんせい、きょうの　クラブは　なんじですか。
クラブは　ごご　三じはんです。

6

Answer the questions in Japanese according to the schedule.

a テニスは　なんじですか。
_____

b バレーボールは　なんじですか。
_____

c ひる休みは　なんじですか。
_____

d やきゅうは　なんじですか。
_____

e バスケットボールは　なんじですか。
_____

スポーツの　日

ごぜん	9：00	バスケットボール
	10：00	サッカー
	11：30	バレーボール
ごご	12：30	ひる休み
	1：00	テニス
	2：00	やきゅう
	3：00	ラグビー

7

Look at the pictures and work out what each person is saying in Japanese. Write these sentences in your exercise book and then practise with a partner.

8

Before you listen to the recording, study the activities in the pictures. As you listen, write the dialogue number next to the appropriate picture.

9

This game known as Blockbusters, is played in pairs. Each student will need a different coloured pen. Toss a dice to decide who starts the game. To win, each person must complete a line (horizontally, vertically or diagonally) of three squares by correctly making sentences according to the picture cues. When the sentence has been said correctly, the person colours the square with his/her coloured pen. It is also important to try to block your partner's progress. To do this, choose a square which will block your partner's path.

10

Read the following messages and then note them below in English.

さなえさん、

きょう がっこうの あとで いっしょに
日本ごの しゅくだいを しましょう。
四じに ぼくの うちに きてください。
いっしょに としょかんに
いきましょう。でんわ してください。
でんわばんごうは ６４０−３９８２
です。

ベン

十ねんせいコンサート
十月二十二日。ごご 一じはん。
がっこうの コンサートです。
十ねんせいの ロックバンドを
ききましょう。

Message: _____

_____

_____

_____

_____

_____

_____

_____

To: _____

From: _____

Message: _____

_____

_____

_____

_____

_____

11

You could work with a partner to proceed through the maze from スタート to ゴール using the picture cues to make sentences in Japanese. All your sentences should end in ましょう.

コーラを　のみましょう。

_____

_____

_____

_____

_____

_____

_____

_____

_____

12

Highlight the matching English and Japanese equivalents.
Use a different colour for each pair.

I won't
Won't you
I did   do
Let's
I will

ます
ました
ません
ませんか
ましょう

I WON'T …

Part A

Think about what activity is being suggested in each picture before you listen to the recording. As you listen to each statement, number the appropriate speech bubble.

Part B

With a partner, say in Japanese what activity is being suggested.

In pairs, practise inviting and responding according to each of the activities in Task 13. The following sample may help you:

ナオミさん、アイスクリームを　たべませんか。
はい、たべましょう。*or*　アイスクリームは　ちょっと...

Read each invitation and then fill in the details in English.

When writing letters、 へ and より mean "to …" and "from …"

a ニッキーさんへ、
金曜日は　日本ごの　テストですね。
いっしょに　べんきょうしませんか。
としょかんに　いきましょう。
エミリー　より。

To:
From: *Nicki*
When: _____
Where: _____
Request: _____
_____

b 九ねんせいの　せんせいへ、
ロックの　バンドを　ききませんか。
コンサートを　します。
スクールホールに　きてください。
コンサートは　三じです。
九ねんせい　より。

To:
From: _____
When: _____
Where: _____
Request: _____
_____

c 八ねんせいへ、
五月二十三日は　がっこうの　日本ごの　日です。
日本ごの　クラスは　すしパーティーを　します。
すしを　たべませんか。
おちゃを　のみましょう。
ともだちと　きてください。
日本ごの　せんせい　より。

To:
From: _____
When: _____
Where: _____
Request: _____
_____

d ようこさんへ、
月曜日は　ゆみさんの　たんじょう日です。
よしくんと　レストランに　いきます。
ようこさんも　きませんか。
パーティーは　ごご　六じはんです。
でんわしてください。
でんわ　ばんごうは　９４３６−５５８２です。
ゆうすけ　より。

To:
From: _____
When: _____
Where: _____
Request: _____
_____

16

You are planning a birthday party. Write an invitation in Japanese. The invitations in the previous task may help you. Don't forget to use ませんか.

17

Before you listen to the recording, discuss with a partner what is happening in the pictures. As you listen to the statements, fill in the time for each activity. Include *am* or *pm* where appropriate.

a *8.00 pm*

b _____

c _____

d _____

e _____

f _____

g _____

h _____

18

BLM 1.1 (Noughts and Crosses) Ask your teacher for the instructions.

Part A

The camp schedule is out of sequence. Number the boxes in correct order from the earliest activity to the latest.

Part B

Now that you have put the activities of the camp schedule in order, note this in English in the table.

日本ごの　キャンプ

☐ ごぜん　八じはんに　バスに　のります。

☐ 十二じに　やきとりと　ごはんを　たべましょう。おいしいですよ。

☐ ごご　三じはんに　日本の　CDを　ききます。

☐ ごぜん　八じに　がっこうに　きてください。

☐ ごご　六じに　日本ごの　てがみを　かきます。

☐ ごご　七じはんに　カラオケを　します。日本の　うたを　うたいませんか。

☐ ごご　一じに　すもうの　ビデオを　みましょう。

☐ ごぜん　十じはんに　日本ごの　ゲームを　します。

☐ ごご　五じに　やきそばを　たべます。それから、おちゃを　のみます。

Time	Activity
_____	_____
_____	_____
_____	_____
_____	_____
_____	_____
_____	_____
_____	_____
_____	_____
_____	_____

Complete the sentences according to your own schedule.

a ごぜん　七じはんに _____

b ごぜん　八じはんに _____

c ごご　一じに _____

d ごご　四じはんに _____

e ごご　六じに _____

21

In Japanese, write a message to a friend suggesting an activity. First, read the example below.

アリシアさんへ、
日曜日に　えいがを　みましょう。
こわい　えいがですよ。
えいがの　あとで　ピザを
たべましょう。
なんじに　いきましょうか。
でんわしてください。
　　ゆうこ　より

Message: _____
_____
_____
_____
_____
_____
_____
_____
_____
_____
_____

22

Part A

Listen to the recording and number the pictures in the order you hear the statements.

Part B

In pairs, practise suggesting and responding to an activity at the places in the pictures.

a

b

c

 d

 e

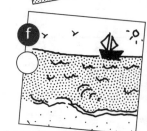 f

 g

 h

 i

 j

23

Ask your partner five questions with どこで and another five questions with なんじに. Each question is worth one point. Record your partner's score below. The example may help you.

どこで　かいものを　しますか。　　　デパートで　かいものを　します。

Score: _____ /10

Part A

Read the passage and answer the questions in English.

> わたしの　かぞくは　五人です。土曜日に　おかあさんは　まちで　かいものを
> します。おとうさんと　ぼくは　こうえんで　サッカーを　します。おにいさんは
> ゲームセンターで　ともだちに　あいます。コンピューターゲームを　します。
> いもうとは　ともだちの　うちで　テレビを　みます。

Who am I talking about? _____

How many people are mentioned? _____

What relation are they to me? _____

List all the different activities everyone does. _____

_____

Part B

Read the passage about Tim and fill in his weekly schedule in English.

Day	Place	Activity
Monday		
	at the park	
		don't play sport
Thursday		
	in town	
Sat/Sun		

> ぼくの　なまえは　ティムです。カナダから
> きました。ちゅうがく三ねんせいです。
> 十五さいです。スポーツが　すきです。
> 月曜日は　がっこうで　バスケットボールを
> します。火曜日は　こうえんで　クリケットを
> します。水曜日は　スポーツを　しません。
> がっこうの　あとは　ひまです。木曜日は
> としょかんで　しゅくだいを　します。
> 金曜日の　ばんは　まちで　ともだちと
> えいがを　みます。土曜日と　日曜日は
> うちで　ともだちと　たのしい　ゲームを
> します。

In Japanese, write an activity you might do at each of these places.

木曜日に　まちで　　　　　かいものを　します。_____

きょう　こうえんで　_____

やまで　_____

二じに　えいがかんで　_____

あした　えんそくで　_____

キャンプで　_____

土曜日に　ともだちの　うちで　_____

ゲームセンターで　_____

26

Listen to the recording and fill in the details in English.

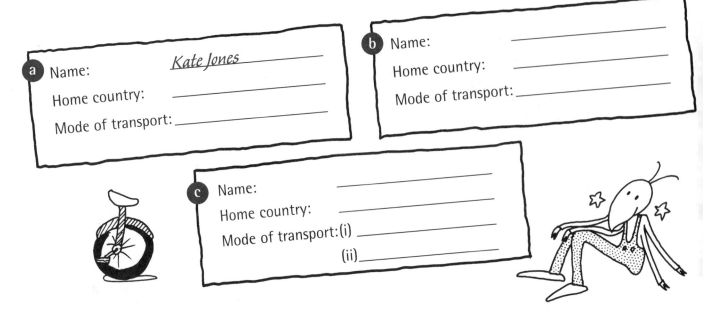

a Name: _Kate Jones_

Home country: _____

Mode of transport: _____

b Name: _____

Home country: _____

Mode of transport: _____

c Name: _____

Home country: _____

Mode of transport: (i) _____

(ii) _____

27

Interview four members of your class to complete the sentences. Use the question
なんで　〜に　いきますか using the places given below.

a せんせい _____ は くるま _____ で　がっこうに　いきます。

b _____ は _____ で　プールに　いきます。

c _____ は _____ で　えいがかんに　いきます。

d _____ は _____ で　としょかんに　いきます。

e _____ は _____ で　ともだちの　うちに　いきます。

28

Match the questions and answers. Write the appropriate number in the bracket.

a いま　なんじですか。 　　　　　(3)　　はい、いきます。 　　　　　　(1)

b なんで　いきましょうか。 　　　(　)　　じてんしゃで　いきましょう。 (2)

c なんじに　いきましょうか。 　　(　)　　四じはんです。 　　　　　　　(3)

d わたしの　パーティーに　きませんか。 (　)　こうえんに　いきましょう。 (4)

e どこで　かいましょうか。 　　　(　)　　七じはんに　いきましょう。 (5)

f なにを　しましょうか。 　　　　(　)　　デパートで　かいましょう。 (6)

29

In pairs, read the dialogue and answer TRUE (T) or FALSE (F) for the following statements.

a Ken is asking Emiko out to a movie (__)

b Emiko does not accept straight away. (__)

c It is 1.00 pm at the moment. (__)

d Ken and Emiko will go to the park at 2.00 pm. (__)

e Before going to the park, Ken and Emiko will go to a friend's house. (__)

f Ken and Emiko will ride their bikes at the park. (__)

g Ken and Emiko will walk to the restaurant. (__)

h Ken gets upset with Emiko. (__)

ケン： えみこさん、ぼくと こうえんに いきませんか。

えみこ： そうですね。なんじに？

ケン： ええと... いま ごご 一じですね。いっしょに ピザハウスで ひるごはんを たべましょう。それから、 二じはんに こうえんに いきましょう。

えみこ： そうね。でも... こうえんで なにを しますか。

ケン： ローラーブレードを しましょう。 いきませんか。

えみこ： そうね。でも... なんで いきますか。

ケン： レストランに あるいて いきます。 それから こうえんに ローラーブレードで いきませんか。 いっしょに いきましょう。

えみこ： そうね。わたしは ちょっと...

ケン： えみこさん！

30

Use the pictures to write each sentence below in Japanese.

a 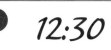 +  +  + いきましょう。

十二じはんに ちかてつで まちに いきましょう。

b  + + 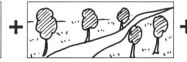 + いきましょう。

c 7:00 +  +  + いきましょう。

d 4:00 + + DEPARTMENT STORE SALE + いきましょう。

e 11:00 + + + いきませんか。

f Monday + + + いきましょう。

g Friday + TAXI + MOVIE THEATRE + いきませんか。

h Wednesday + + GAME CENTRE + いきましょう。

i 18th January + + + いきましょう。

j 6th August + + + いきましょう。

31 👀

In pairs, prepare a dialogue in your exercise books in which you arrange to do an activity. You should be able to enact your dialogue in front of the class. Include the following details: date, time, place and how to get there.

Complete the crossword by inserting the appropriate verb or word.

よこ Across

2 あたらしい　本を＿＿＿＿＿＿＿＿ (buy)

4 CDを＿＿＿＿＿＿＿＿＿＿＿ (listen)

5 サンドイッチを＿＿＿＿＿＿＿ (eat)

7 パーティーに ＿＿＿＿＿＿＿＿ (go)

8 ジュースを ＿＿＿＿＿＿＿＿＿ (drink)

9 まんがを＿＿＿＿＿＿＿＿＿ (read)

たて Down

1 パンケーキを ＿＿＿＿＿＿＿＿ (make)

2 てがみを＿＿＿＿＿＿＿＿＿ (write)

3 ＿＿＿＿＿＿＿＿なんじですか。(now)

6 日本ごを＿＿＿＿＿＿＿＿＿ (study)

8 バスに ＿＿＿＿＿＿＿＿＿＿ (ride)

Search for the following words. The words can be found horizontally, vertically and diagonally. The same letter can be used more than once.

どこあスポーツおとき
テレビしえでなくもサ
ニいうピたんんけだン
スむだれクわじしちド
おがっこうニセねゃイ
いもうとソヌっヘッ
つタおにいさんクみチ
ちマねベコンサートほ
バスえニんのらひーき
でなさいおとうとスょ
にほんにごトうはトう
ジュースひるごはんめ

bus	juice	picnic	telephone	tomorrow	who?
concert	lunch	sandwich	television	train	younger brother
English	lunch box	school	tennis	what time?	younger sister
friend	older brother	sea	toast	when?	
Japan	older sister	sports	today	where?	

おべんとう　クイズ

1 Circle the correct answer.

a When someone asks you なんじですか they want to know:
- what day it is.
- ✓ what time it is.
- what age you are.

b When you want to suggest to your friend to watch a movie, you say:
- ✓ えいがに　いきましょう。
- えいがに　いきました。
- えいがに　いきません。

c When you want to invite your friend to your party, you say:
- ✓ パーティーに　いきますか。
- パーティーに　いきましょう。
- パーティーに　きませんか。

d If someone tells you コンサートは
ーじはんです:
- s/he is saying the concert is at one o'clock.
- ✓ s/he is saying the concert is at half past one.
- s/he is saying the movie is number one.

e If someone replies to your invitation, saying あしたは　ちょっと . . . s/he means:
- ✓ s/he can't go tomorrow.
- tomorrow is a short day.
- tomorrow sounds good.

f If your friend said なんで　日本に　いきますか how would you answer most appropriately?
- ちかてつで　いきます。
- しんかんせんで　いきます。
- ✓ ひこうきで　いきます。

g げんきでね is used when:
- someone can't wait to see you again.
- ✓ someone is asking how you are.
- someone says take care of yourself.

h How would you say 'I'm embarrassed'?
- さびしいです。
- たのしみです。
- ✓ はずかしいです。

i If your friend said ひっこしを　します s/he means:
- s/he has hiccups.
- s/he is making a phone call.
- ✓ s/he is moving house.

j If you see けんいち　より written on an invitation, it means:
- ✓ it's from Kenichi.
- it's to Kenichi.
- it's about Kenichi.

2 Circle the odd word in each row.

a なんじ　どこで　なんで　(まち)
b バス　くるま　じてんしゃ　(コンサート)
c としょかん　(ともだち)　デパート　うち

3 Insert the correct particle に、を or で in each bracket.

a ちかてつ (で) まち (に) いきましょう
b 三じ (に) えいが (に) みましょう。
c 五じはん (に) うち (＿) しゅくだい
(＿) しましょう。
d きょう、ごぜん　十じ (に) くるま
(で) こうえん (に) いきました。

4 Answer the following questions in Japanese.

a いま　なんじですか。
七時です。

b なんじに　がっこうに　いきますか。
八時です

c 土曜日に　としょかんで　うたを
うたいませんか。
＿＿＿＿＿＿＿＿＿＿

d なんで　えいがかんに　いきますか。
くるまで　いきましょう。

e なんじに　しゅくだいを　しましょうか。
午後八時です

unit 2

でんわしてね

1

Listen to the テレフォンサービス to find out the exact time. Write it below in English. Include *am* or *pm*.

a *2:15 pm*

b _____

c _____

d _____

e _____

f _____

g _____

h _____

2

Listen to the times given and number them in the order you hear them.

a 6.10 (_____)

b 4.20 (_____)

c 2.55 (_____)

d 9.25 (_____)

e 7.50 (_____)

f 8.55 (_____)

g 4.05 (*1*)

h 6.55 (_____)

i 12.15 (_____)

j 6.45 (_____)

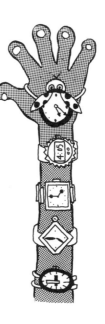

3

Part A

Listen to the recording and circle the correct time.

a 6.10
5.50
8.10

b 25 minutes to 7
a quarter to seven
25 minutes past 7

c 4.15
3.45
3.55

d 8.05
6.55
1.05

e 20 minutes past 10
20 minutes to 11
20 minutes past 12

f 6.35
6.40
7.40

g 15 minutes to 4
15 minutes past 4
25 minutes past 4

h 9.55
10.00
11.00

i 8.45
8.15
8.35

j 10 minutes to 3
10 minutes past 2
10 minutes to 2

Part B

Listen to the times again and note in English what the times are referring to.

a (*dinner*) **b** (_____) **c** (_____) **d** (_____) **e** (_____)

f (_____) **g** (_____) **h** (_____) **i** (_____) **j** (_____)

Part A

In your exercise book, prepare a table of two columns: ばんぐみ and 時かん. Using the television guide, fill in your table with five Japanese programs you would like to watch.

テレビガイド　５月１７日　金曜日		
NHK チャンネル 1	日本テレビ チャンネル　4	7 ジテレビ チャンネル 6
4 00 こどもの　テレビ 　　　「ジャンケンポン」 30 「ポンキッキー」	00 Punchで　デート！ 　　「きょうと　こうこう」	00 スクービードウ 30 シンプソン
5 00 どうぶつえんシリーズ 　　　「メルボルンどうぶつえんに 　　　いきました」	00 クイズ「１００人に 　　ききました」 45 ヤング　タレント　タイム	00 ツグラッツ
6 00 ケロッピ 30 バツマル	00 おもしろい、へんな　ビデオ 　　「こんな　ビデオを 　　とりました」	00 スーパータイム　ゴジラ 55 てんきよほう
7 00 NHK ニュース 45 ドラマ「りのちゃん」	15 日本で　いちばん 　　おいしい　レストラン	05 プロやきゅう 　　ヤクルトカップ

Part B

Without looking at the television guide, ask your partner what time your selected programs begin by saying ～は　何時ですか。Your partner checks the television guide and tells you in Japanese the time the program begins. You write the time in the 時かん column. Then swap roles.

5

Read the passage and answer the questions in English.

わたしの　いちにち

わたしの　かぞくは　四人です。おとうさんと　おかあさんと　いもうとと　わたしです。まいにち　七時半に　あさごはんを　たべます。でも、おとうさんは　あさごはんを　たべません。おとうさんは　七時十五分まえに　くるまで　まちに　いきます。わたしと　いもうとは　でんしゃで　がっこうに　いきます。まいにち　八時五分の　でんしゃに　のります。がっこうで　一時十分に　ひるごはんを　たべます。火曜日の　ひる休みは　十二時半です。火曜日は　スポーツの　日です。水曜日に　バンドの　れんしゅうを　します。四時二十分まえです。がっこうの　あとで　四時に　しゅくだいを　します。それから、五時半に　テレビの　コメディーを　みます。10チャンネルです。ときどき　おもしろい　まんがも　みます。月曜日の　五時十五分まえに　やきゅうの　れんしゅうを　します。そして、木曜日の　四時四十分に　ピアノの　レッスンに　いきます。まいばん　九時半に　ねます。

V ねます go to bed

Part A

a. I eat breakfast at _____7:30_____ .

b. My father leaves home at _____7:15_____ .

c. I catch the train at _____8:05_____ .

d. At school I eat lunch at _____1:10_____ except on _____Tuesday_____ when I eat at _____12:30_____ .

e. On Wednesday, I have band practice at _____4:20_____

f. After school I do homework at _____4:00_____ and watch T.V. at _____5:30_____ .

g. On _____Monday_____ at _____5:~~10~~ 5:15_____ I practise baseball and on _____Thursday_____ at _____4:40_____ I have a piano lesson.

h. I go to bed at _____9:30_____ .

Part B

a. At 6.45am, my father _____

b. At 7.30am, I _____eat breakfast_____

c. At 8.05, I _____catch train_____

d. At 1.10, _____I eat lunch_____

e. At 3.40, I _____

f. At 5.30, I _____watch TV_____

g. At 4.45 on Mondays, I _____am doing_____

h. At 4.40 on Thursdays, I _____have piano lesson_____

i. At 9.30, I _____go to bed_____

Part C

a. How many people are in the family? List the family members.

_____4, father, mother, younger sister_____

b. Who eats breakfast and who doesn't?

_____The author does, his father does not._____

c. How does the writer get to school?

_____train_____

d Why does the writer mention two different lunch times?

Tuesday is their sports day

e What does the writer do after she has done her homework? Explain in detail.

He ~~does~~ does homework at 4:00 and then watch T.V.

f The writer has three special activities in the week. What are they and when do they take place?

1 Activity: _piano lesson_   When: _Thursday 4:40_

2 Activity: _baseball practice_   When: _Monday 5:45_

3 Activity: _ban practice_)   When: _Wendesday 4:20_

6

Fill in the missing times to best describe your day.

a _七時_   に あさごはんを たべます。

b _八時_   に がっこうに いきます。

c _午後十二時四十五分_   に ひるごはんを たべます。

d _午後四時半_   に うちに かえります。

e _午後八時_   に しゅくだいを します。

f _午後十一時_   に テレビを みます。

7

Complete the sentences in Japanese with an activity you do at the appropriate time.

a 四時に _宿題を します。_

b 五時に _____

c 六時半に _ねます_

d 七時に _晩ご飯を食べます。_

e 八時半に _八時_

8

Write a schedule of what you did last weekend. Include times and activities.

しゅうまつに　何を　しましたか。	
土曜日	日曜日

9

> In Japan, O（まる）is used for True and X（ばつ）is used for False

Listen to the conversations in which students are talking about what they did or didn't do last week. Write (O) for something that **was** done, or (X) for something that **was not** done.

a ――――――― b ――――――― c ――――――― d ――――――― e ―――――――

f ――――――― g ――――――― h ――――――― i ――――――― j ―――――――

10

Interview your class members to find out who has done each of the following activities. If someone has done the activity, ask them to put their initials next to the appropriate activity. You must not ask the same person twice.

a しゅうまつに　ともだちと　でかけました。　　　　　　　_____

b おもしろい　えいがを　みました。　　　　　　　　　　　_____

c ともだちの　しゃしんを　とりました。　　　　　　　　　_____

d きのう、ボーイフレンド／ガールフレンドに　でんわを　しました。　_____

e きょう、あさごはんに　コーンフレークを　たべました。　_____

f まちで　かいものを　しました。　　　　　　　　　　　　_____

g パーティーに　いきました。　　　　　　　　　　　　　　_____

h 土曜日に　レストランに　いきました。　　　　　　　　　_____

i きょう　Eメールを　かきました。　　　　　　　　　　　_____

j きのう、あるいて　がっこうに　きました。　　　　　　　_____

BLM 2.1 *(Murder mystery)* Ask your teacher for the instructions.

12

Match the sentence and the picture by writing the appropriate letter.

a がっこうで　しゃしんを　とりました。

b ともだちに　でんわを　しました。

c こうえんで　ボートに　のりました。

d デパートで　かいものを　しました。

e としょかんで　しゅくだいを　しました。

13

Here is a picture of some of the *Obentoo* students on an えんそく. Read the sentences and write **(O)** (まる) or **(X)** (ばつ) in the brackets according to the picture. If the sentence is not correct, rewrite it correctly.

a ベンくんは　チョコレートアイスクリームを　たべました。　　　　　（＿＿＿）

b けんいちくんは　ゆきさんと　さなえさんの　ビデオを　とりました。　（＿＿＿）

c たかこさんは　ともだちと　ボートに　のりました。　　　　　　　　（＿＿＿）

d しんごくんは　うたを　うたいました。　　　　　　　　　　　　　　（＿＿＿）

e すずきせんせいは　がっこうで　でんわを　しました。　　　　　　　（＿＿＿）

_____

_____

_____

_____

14

Read the dialogues and answer the questions in English.

a **A:** ゆうこさん、きのう　テストを　しましたか。

B: はい、フランスごの　テストを　しました。

What did the person do yesterday?_____

b **A:** たかしくん、月曜日に　せんせいに　でんわを　しましたか。

B: はい、しました。でも、せんせいは　いませんでした。

What did Takashi do? _____

When?_____

What problem did he find?_____

c **A:** だいすけくん、しゅくだいを　しましたか。

B: いいえ、しませんでした。ともだちと　でかけました。

What should Daisuke have done?_____

What did he do instead?_____

d **A:** おかあさん、きょう、かいものを　しましたか。

B: ううん、しませんでしたよ。あした　します。

Who is the person talking to? _____

What did s/he ask? _____

What was the answer? _____

e **A:** じゅんくん、日曜日に　まちに　いきました。

B: ちかてつに　のりましたか。

A: ううん、ちかてつに　のりませんでした。バスで　いきました。

When did Jun go to town?_____

What transport alternatives does he have? _____

f **A:** 土曜日に　こうえんで　ゆきさんと　あいましたか。

B: ええ、あいましたよ。ゆきさんは　いつも　いぬと　いっしょに
こうえんに　きます。

Where was he on Saturday? _____

What was Yuki doing? _____

g **A:** 火曜日に　日本の　えいがを　みましたか。

B: ええ、ひる休みに　としょかんで　みました。

What day is mentioned?_____

What did she do in the library? _____

When? _____

h **A:** みちこさん、カラオケボックスで　うたを　うたいましたか。

B: いいえ、うたいませんでした。はずかしい。

What wouldn't Michiko do? _____

Why? _____

i **A:** きのう、ひるごはんに　スパゲッティを　たべましたか。

B: ええ、たべました。スパゲッティが　だいすきです。

What did he eat? _____

When? _____

15

Write a sentence in Japanese to describe each picture. You should write *did not do* not for pictures *b* and *e*.

_____

_____

_____

_____

16

Write the following sentences in **hiragana** to find out the hidden message. The circled letters will form a sentence when placed in the grid below.

a I took a photo.　　し　ゃ　し　ん　を　と　り　ま　し　た。

b Let's ride a bike.

c I didn't go to school.

d I did some shopping.

e It is 4.30.

f I didn't watch TV.

g I made a phone call.

h I will do my homework.

i Let's go on Thursday.

j I sang a song.

17

Listen to the ten sentences and highlight the correct time in each row.

a	today	tomorrow	yesterday	last week
b	this week	last week	next week	next year
c	last month	next month	last week	this month
d	next year	next month	this year	last year
e	today	this week	this month	this year
f	yesterday	last week	last month	last year
g	tomorrow	next week	next month	next year
h	this week	last year	last week	this month
i	today	next year	next month	yesterday
j	tomorrow	last week	next month	this year

18

Part A
Look at the pictures and from the list below, write down when you did or you will do the activities. Use all the time words in the list.

いつ　しますか

Part B
Using the pictures, with a partner, practise asking いつ　〜を　しますか。 or responding with the time word you have inserted.

きのう、きょう、あした、せんしゅう、こんしゅう、らいしゅう、
せんげつ、こんげつ、らいげつ、きょねん、ことし、らいねん

19

Read the Japanese statements and mark (T) *True* or (F) *False* beside the English equivalent.

a. あした　じてんしゃに　のりましょう。 　　Let's ride our bikes tomorrow. 　　(___)

b. らいしゅう　でんわを　します。 　　I'll telephone you next week. 　　(___)

c. せんげつ　うみに　いきました。 　　He went in to town last month. 　　(___)

d. らいねん　日本に　いきます。 　　I'll go to Japan this year. 　　(___)

e. きのう　うたを　うたいました。 　　I sang a song today. 　　(___)

f. きょねん　えいがを　みませんでした。 　　I didn't see any movies last year. 　　(___)

g. らいげつ　どうぶつえんに　いきましょう。 　　Let's go to the zoo next month. 　　(___)

h. こんしゅうの　金曜日に　テニスを　しましょう。 　　Let's play tennis on Thursday this week. (___)

i. きのう　かいものを　しませんでした。 　　I didn't go shopping yesterday. 　　(___)

j. いつ　パーティーに　いきましたか。　せんしゅう　いきました。 　　When did you go to the party? I went last week. 　　(___)

20

Read the passage and answer the questions in English.

きょうは　休みでした。がっこうに　いきませんでした。あさ　九時半に　こうえんで　ともだちに　あいました。いっしょに　じてんしゃに　のりました。そして、ひるごはんの　あとで　ともだちの　うちに　いきました。うちで　テレビを　みました。

あしたも　休みです。いいですね！こんばん　ともだちに　でんわを　します。あした　いっしょに　でかけます。十一時に　まちに　いきます。それから、えいがを　みます。ぼくは　休みが　だいすきです。

a. Which days is he talking about? _____

b. Why is he so happy? _____

c. What are his plans for the first day? _____

d. What are his plans for the second day? _____

21

If you need to, write down the equivalent hiragana words and then search for them in the puzzle. The words can be found in any direction and some letters may be used twice. Use the remaining letters from the puzzle to complete the phrase below.

き	の	う	こ	が	ん	ぜ	ご	す	ら
ょ	ん	き	ん	よ	う	び	ご	い	い
う	ら	い	げ	つ	こ	と	し	よ	ね
こ	ば	り	つ	ま	げ	ゅ	し	う	ん
ん	ね	よ	き	つ	う	ん	た	び	び
し	に	ち	よ	う	び	お	せ	め	う
ゅ	で	う	ど	じ	よ	び	と	た	よ
う	び	う	に	ゅ	か	う	し	じ	く
せ	ん	し	ゅ	う	か	あ	じ	か	も

yesterday	this week	next month	Sunday	Thursday	pm	5.00
today	next week	last year	Monday	Friday	when	9.00
tomorrow	last month	this year	Tuesday	Saturday	2.00	
last week	this month	next year	Wednesday	am	4.00	

22

Answer following questions in Japanese.

a あした 何で がっこうに いきますか。

_____

b きょう 何を たべましたか。

_____

c きのう 何を べんきょうしましたか。

_____

d せんげつ ともだちと うみに いきましたか。

_____

e らいねん 日本ごを べんきょうしますか。

_____

23

Write the following sentences in Japanese.

a I will write a letter next week.

_____

b Last year I went to Japan.

_____

c This month is March.

_____

d I telephoned my friend today.

_____

e Tomorrow we will make sushi at school.

_____

24

Part A

Listen to the recording and write the number next to the matching picture.

Part B

Listen to the recording again to complete the following sentences.

a Yesterday I went to _____a restaurant_____ with _my uncle and aunt_ .

b I _____ with _____ .

c _____ will _____ with _____ .

d I _____ with _____ at the _____ .

e Yesterday I _____ with _____ .

25 🔊 📝

Listen to the recording and answer the following questions in English.

a 1 Who is Yoosuke talking to?

_____

2 Who did he go to the baseball with?

_____

b 1 What are they looking at?

_____

2 What can they see Yoosuke doing? Who with?

_____

c 1 When does Yoosuke want to go shopping?

_____

2 How is he planning to get there?

_____

3 Is he going alone?

_____

d 1 What does Yoosuke suggest to Mieko?

_____

2 What is Mieko's response?

_____

3 Why does Yoosuke get into trouble with Mieko?

_____

Ask five people the following questions and record his/her answers. Write the most popular answer below.

a 日曜日に　何を　しましたか。＿＿＿＿＿＿＿＿＿＿＿＿＿＿＿＿

だれと　しましたか。＿＿＿＿＿＿＿＿＿＿＿＿＿＿＿＿＿＿＿＿

b きのう、おもしろい　テレビの　ばんぐみを　みましたか。＿＿＿＿＿＿＿＿

何を　みましたか。＿＿＿＿＿＿＿＿＿＿＿＿＿＿＿＿＿＿＿＿

だれと　みましたか。＿＿＿＿＿＿＿＿＿＿＿＿＿＿＿＿＿＿＿

c きょう、だれと　がっこうに　きましたか。＿＿＿＿＿＿＿＿＿＿＿＿

d きょう、がっこうの　あとで、何を　しますか。＿＿＿＿＿＿＿＿＿＿

だれと　しますか。＿＿＿＿＿＿＿＿＿＿＿＿＿＿＿＿＿＿＿＿

e ひまなときに　何を　しますか。＿＿＿＿＿＿＿＿＿＿＿＿＿＿＿

だれと　しますか。＿＿＿＿＿＿＿＿＿＿＿＿＿＿＿＿＿＿＿＿

The most popular answer: ＿＿＿＿＿＿＿＿＿＿＿＿＿＿＿＿＿＿＿＿

Choose one word from each column to make up the five sentences. The same word should not be used twice.

きょう	おとうとと	としょかんで	がっこうに	いきました
せんしゅう	あかあさんと	うみで	かいものを	しました
きょねん	ともだちと	まちで	サーフィンを	みました
せんげつ	一人で	カラオケボックスで	ビデオを	しました
おひるごはんの あとで	かぞくと	でんしゃで	日本の　うたを	うたいました

a きょう　おとうとと　うみで　サーフィンを　しました。＿＿＿＿＿

b ＿＿＿＿＿＿＿＿＿＿＿＿＿＿＿＿＿＿＿＿＿＿＿＿＿＿＿＿

c ＿＿＿＿＿＿＿＿＿＿＿＿＿＿＿＿＿＿＿＿＿＿＿＿＿＿＿＿

d ＿＿＿＿＿＿＿＿＿＿＿＿＿＿＿＿＿＿＿＿＿＿＿＿＿＿＿＿

e ＿＿＿＿＿＿＿＿＿＿＿＿＿＿＿＿＿＿＿＿＿＿＿＿＿＿＿＿

f ＿＿＿＿＿＿＿＿＿＿＿＿＿＿＿＿＿＿＿＿＿＿＿＿＿＿＿＿

Look at the diary grid and use the picture to write a sentence for each day. Include all the details given. Make up your own sentence where there is no picture.

Four students are talking about what they did on the weekend. Listen to the recording and fill in the table in English.

どうでしたか				
What?	When?	Where?	Who with?	How was it?
a *ice-skating*	*Sunday*		*friend*	*cold*
b				
c				
d				

BLM 2.2 (ゲーム：どうでしたか) Ask your teacher for the game instructions.

31

Read the article Takako wrote for her school newsletter and mark (T) *True* or (F) *False* in the brackets.

チーズ！

わたしは　もりやま　たかこです。せんげつ　オーストラリアに
いきました。

十二月二十七日の、八時四十分の　ひこうきに　のりました。
カンタスの　ひこうきは　とても　よかったです。エマさんと
エマさんの　かぞくに　あいました。エマさんの　おにいさんは
とても　やさしかったです。

二十九日に　エマさんと　いっしょに　どうぶつえんに
いきました。コアラと　カンガルーの　ビデオを　とりました。
どうぶつえんは　あつかったです。

十二月三十一日に　エマさんの　うちで　パーティーを
しました。バーベキューを　しました。とても
おいしかったです。エマさんの　おかあさんは　とても
いそがしかったです。たくさん　CDを　ききました。
エマさんと　日本の　うたも　うたいました。オーストラリアの
パーティーは　とても　おもしろかったです。

a Takako went to Australia last year. (_____)

b Takako didn't enjoy her trip in the aeroplane. (_____)

c Takako met Emma and Emma's family. (_____)

d Takako took photos of koalas, kangaroos and emus at the zoo. (_____)

e On 31st December, Takako went to a beach party. (_____)

f Emma's mother was very busy. (_____)

Where a Japanese clue has been given, provide the Japanese for the **opposite** word. Where an English clue has been given, write the equivalent Japanese.

よこ
2 was good
4 was embarrassing
5 つまらなかった
7 was fun
8 やすかった

たて
1 やさしかった
3 おいしかった
5 ちいさかった
6 さむかった

In your exercise book, write a diary entry for one week. Include your thoughts about the activities you did.

Using Takako's article as a guide, in your exercise book, write an article about a recent experience (include details such as when, where, who with and your impressions).

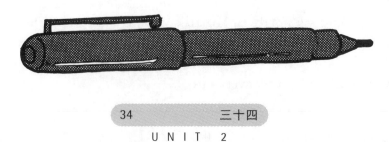

Follow the path to find out who, when, who s/he did the activities with and what activities s/he did. Also describe what the activity was like. Write the information in complete Japanese sentences. Be careful of the particle に!

a けんいちくんは　きのう　ちえこさんと　コーラを　のみました。おいしかったです。

b _____

_____

c _____

_____

d _____

_____

e _____

_____

f _____

_____

おべんとう　クイズ

1 Circle the correct answer.

  a When someone says 一時五分まえです, it means:
- five minutes to seven.
- five minutes past one.
- five minutes to one.

  b If your friend said to you まちに いきました:
- she is inviting you to go to town.
- she is telling you she is going to go to town.
- she is telling you she went to town.

  c If you are asked でんわを　しましたか, how would you answer?
- いいえ、しません。
- いいえ、しませんでした。

  d If you have a test this week, you would say:
- こんしゅう　テストを　します。
- せんしゅう　テストを　しました。
- らいしゅう　テストを　します。

  e If you did your homework with Shingo, you would say:
- しんごくんの　しゅくだいを　しました。
- しんごくんと　しゅくだいを　しました。
- しんごくんは　しゅくだいを　しました。

  f If your friend said すごい！s/he means:
- oh!
- wow!
- you're kidding!

  g How do you say hello in Japanese on the phone?
- ああ、もう。
- もしもし。
- もっともっと。

2 Draw a line to connect the Japanese time word and its corresponding word in English.

あした	yesterday
きのう	today
きょう	tomorrow
こんしゅう	last week
せんしゅう	this week
らいしゅう	next week
せんげつ	last month
らいげつ	this month
こんげつ	next month
ことし	last year
きょねん	this year
らいねん	next year

3 Give the antonyms *(opposite)* for the following adjectives.

  a おおきかった   _____

  b まずかった   _____

  c おもしろかった   _____

  d さむかった   _____

  e やすかった   _____

  f むずかしかった   _____

4 Complete the sentences using the hints given. Where there are no hints, write your own word.

  a いま _____ ですか。(what time？)

    _____ です。(9.05)

  b _____ かいものに　いきましたか。(with whom？)

    _____ いきました。(with my uncle)

  c こうえんで _____ しましたか。(what？)

    こうえんで　ボートに _____ 。

  d きのうは _____ でしたか。

    きのうは _____ です。(busy)

  e らいしゅう　日本ごの　クラスで ビデオを _____ 。(watch)

  f せんしゅう　ともだちと　まちに _____ 。(went)

  g きのう　かいものを _____ 。

  h あした　しゅくだいを _____ 。

5 Answer the questions in Japanese.

  a きょねん　日本ごを べんきょうしましたか。

    _____

  b ことし　クラスの　しゃしんを とりましたか。

    _____

  c だれと　がっこうに　きましたか。

    _____

  d せんしゅうの　テストは　どうでしたか。

    _____

1

You will hear a number in Japanese, and then an item. Look at the pictures and write the correct number in kanji under each item as you hear it.

a

b

c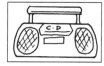

d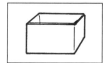

2

Read the following sentences and draw a picture of a room which includes everything mentioned below.

ベッドが あります。
いすが あります。
つくえが あります。
本だなが あります。
おかあさんが います。
ふでばこが あります。

3

Complete these sentences using あります or います.

a けんいちくんが _____

b テレビが _____

c にわが _____

d いもうとが _____

e うちに　ベッドが _____

f へやに　いぬが _____

g がっこうに　本が　たくさん _____

h ともだちの　ペンが _____

i にんじゃは　どこに _____ か。

j 本だなの　中に　アルバムが _____

k テーブルの　上に　でんきスタンドが _____

l にわに　せんせいの　ともだちが _____

m くまの　ぬいぐるみは　どこに _____ か。

4

Hiroshi has left his pen in various locations. Listen to the recording and mark (O) or (X) for each picture.

a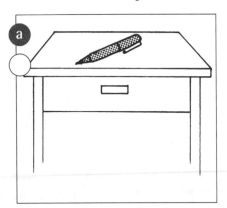

b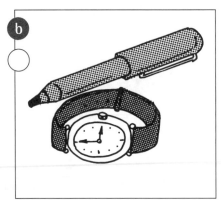

c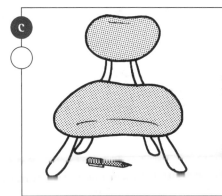

d

e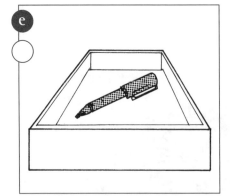

f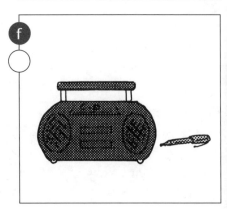

5

In pairs practise asking each other 'Is there a chair?' etc. and answering はい、あります or いいえ、ありません from the information in the picture.

6

Akiko has put many items in different spots in her room. Complete the sentences according to the pictures.

a <u>とけいは　はこの　前に　あります。</u>

b しゃしんは _____

c いぬは _____

d いすは _____

e でんわは_____

a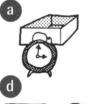
b
c
d
e

7

Using the picture you drew in Task 2, add the following items below. Be sure to draw them in the correct locations! When you have finished, compare your work with a partner.

コンピューターは　どこに　ありますか。	つくえの　上に　あります。
いぬは　どこに　いますか。	いすの　下に　います。
でんきスタンドは　どこに　ありますか。	ベッドの　よこに　あります。
とけいは　どこに　ありますか。	コンピューターの　前に　あります。
てがみは　どこに　ありますか。	ふでばこの　中に　あります。
ぬいぐるみは　どこに　ありますか。	ふでばこの　うしろに　あります。

8

Here is a picture of Michiko and some of her friends. Listen to the recording so that you can fill in each person's name tag.

みちこ

9

BLM 3.1 (Maze game) Ask your teacher for the game instructions.

10

To describe this messy house, write at least ten sentences using います or あります. Practise using both types of verbs.

a つくえの　上に　とけいが　あります。

b _____

c _____

d _____

e _____

f _____

g _____

h _____

i _____

j _____

k _____

Kyoko is talking to her friend on the telephone. She is describing where various items are located. Listen to what Kyoko is saying and tick the picture which matches the description.

12

Find out who owns each of these rooms by listening carefully to the information given on the recording. In English, write the owner's name (さなえ、しんご、ちえこ、ゆうすけ) above each room.

BLM 3.2 (まちがいさがし) (Find the mistakes)
Ask your teacher for the instructions.

14

In pairs, describe your room to each other. As you describe it, your partner will take notes in English in his/her notebook. When you have finished your description, check your partner's work. Then swap roles. Include at least five items in your description.

15

Complete the chart on the next page, filling in as much information as possible in English about each person from the reading passages.

a ひさこ

わたしの うちは さっぽろに あります。さっぽろは さむいです。うまや うしや ひつじなどが たくさん います。がっこうは うちの よこに あります。だから、がっこうに あるいて いきます。わたしの うちは べんりな ところに あります。にわは とても おおきいです。

あるいて walking
ところ place

b まさゆき

ぼくの うちは とうきょうに あります。アパートです。アパートが たくさん あります。だから、にわが ありません。ぼくは がっこうに じてんしゃで いきます。がっこうは しずかな こうえんの よこに あります。とても きれいです。ぼくは がっこうが だいすきです。

だから because of that

c アマンダ

わたしは ニュージーランド人です。いまの うちは とても おおきいです。きれいな にわが あります。わたしの へやに ぬいぐるみが たくさん あります。つくえも あります。でも、べんきょうが きらいです。だから、つくえの 上に ペンだけが ありますよ。きれいでしょう。

だけ only

d ダソ

ぼくの　うちは　アテネに　あります。アテネは　ギリシャで　いちばん　おおきい
まちです。ことしの　なつは　とても　あついです。いま、うちの　中は　あついです。
うちに　せんぷうきと　まどが　たくさん　あります。ちいさい　にわが　あります。

いちばん　おおきい *biggest*
なつ　*summer*
あつい　*hot*
せんぷうき　*electric fan*

Survey chart

	Is it a house or a flat?	Is there a garden?	Where do they live?	List two items in or near the house.
a Hisako				
b Masayuki				
c Amanda				
d Daso				

16

Choose one of the passages from Task 15 to practise reading aloud. Read it several times so that you feel
confident to read it aloud to the class. You might like to record your reading and listen to yourself to
check your pronunciation and fluency. This task may be assessed by your teacher.
BLM Extra 6 (Reading assessment sheet) Ask your teacher for the assessment criteria.

17

Write the Japanese word for each of the following adjectives in the space provided. Then, sort the adjectives into each basket by writing the appropriate letter.

a cold   さむい _____

b new   _____

c clean/pretty   _____

d nice/lovely   _____

e convenient/handy   _____

f big   _____

g spacious   _____

h quiet   _____

i small   _____

j interesting   _____

k cute   _____

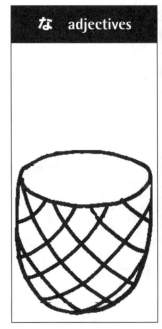

い adjectives   な adjectives

a

18

Revise all the adjectives you know! Describe each of the items using the number of adjectives suggested. Write a full sentence in Japanese in your exercise book. **Do not use the same adjective twice.**

a
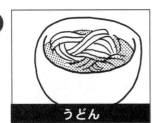
うどん

い adjectives (2)
な adjectives (1)

うどんは　おいしいです。

うどんは　まずいです。

うどんが　すきです。

b
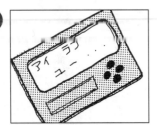

い adjectives (1)
な adjectives (2)

d

い adjectives (3)
な adjectives (2)

c

えみこ

い adjectives (4)
な adjectives (1)

e

ゴジラ

い adjectives (4)
な adjectives (1)

Describe the following pictures by writing a suitable adjective before the nouns.

おおきい ＿＿＿＿＿＿＿＿＿＿ うち

＿＿＿＿＿＿＿＿＿＿ でんきスタンド

＿＿＿＿＿＿＿＿＿＿ いぬ

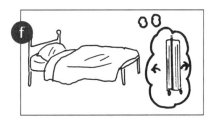

＿＿＿＿＿＿＿＿＿＿ ベッド

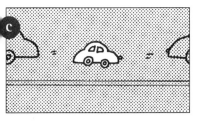

＿＿＿＿＿＿＿＿＿＿ くるま

＿＿＿＿＿＿＿＿＿＿ へや

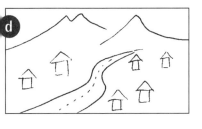

＿＿＿＿＿＿＿＿＿＿ まち

＿＿＿＿＿＿＿＿＿＿ とけい

Choose three of the adjective and noun pairs from Task 19 to make complete sentences in Japanese.

a ＿＿＿＿＿＿＿＿＿＿＿＿＿＿＿＿＿＿＿＿＿＿＿＿＿＿＿＿＿＿＿＿＿＿＿＿＿

b ＿＿＿＿＿＿＿＿＿＿＿＿＿＿＿＿＿＿＿＿＿＿＿＿＿＿＿＿＿＿＿＿＿＿＿＿＿

c ＿＿＿＿＿＿＿＿＿＿＿＿＿＿＿＿＿＿＿＿＿＿＿＿＿＿＿＿＿＿＿＿＿＿＿＿＿

Answer the following questions using あります、
ありません、います or いません accordingly.
The ending you use depends on the question
and the information given in each picture.

> いますandあります
> *are used for "there is…"*
> いませんandありません
> *are used for "there isn't…"*

a いすの　上に　はがきが　ありますか。　　はい、あります。

b はこの　中に　ちいさい　うさぎが　いますか。　＿＿＿＿＿＿＿

c テーブルの　上に　おおきい　本が　ありますか。　＿＿＿＿＿＿＿

d ベッドに　いもうとが　いますか。　＿＿＿＿＿＿＿

e つくえの　下に　コンピューターが　ありますか。　＿＿＿＿＿＿＿

f へやに　さなえさんが　いますか。　＿＿＿＿＿＿＿

g にわに　あひるが　いますか。　＿＿＿＿＿＿＿

h いすの　上に　ねずみが　いますか。　＿＿＿＿＿＿＿

i はこの　中に　ベンくんの　ノートが　ありますか。　＿＿＿＿＿＿＿

Create a picture postcard telling your friends about your new house or your current house (refer to the
sample on page 36 of the Student Book). Set out the card in the correct Japanese way (include your name,
address and the appropriate greeting). Don't forget to add a picture of you at your house on the front of
the postcard.

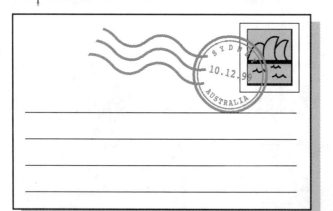

23

In your exercise book, write a letter to an imaginary penfriend in Japan, or if you have a penfriend already, write to her/him. Describe where you live, your room and the different items you have in it. Also remember to include the correct opening and closing phrases. You may wish to refer to pages 37 and 47 of the Student Book.

This may be assessed by your teacher. BLM Extra 7 (Writing assessment sheet) Ask your teacher for the assessment criteria.

24

Rearrange the Japanese words to form a sentence. Check that the meaning corresponds with the English given. *This can be really tricky!*

a There's a watch in the pencil case.
(とけい、の、あります、ふでばこ、に、が、中)

ふでばこの　中に　とけいが　あります。

b There's a new computer on the desk.
(つくえ、が、コンピューター、に、あたらしい、上、あります、の)

つくえの

c Next to my room there is a toilet.
(トイレ、へや、わたしの、の、に、あります、よこ、が)

d There are lots of boxes under the Christmas tree.
(が、あります、下、クリスマスツリー、はこ、たくさん、に、の)

e Kenichi's house is in front of the school.
(がっこう、前、の、あります、けんいちくんの、に、うち、が)

f It's very cold. Sanae is in front of the heater.
(です、とても、さむい)（の、います、さなえさん、は、に、前、ヒーター)

Search for the words in the list below. When you have found all the words, there will be some remaining letters which spell a message. The words you are looking for exist horizontally, vertically and diagonally downwards. There will be some letters which overlap.

✳Note: there are two overlapping words which use よ: in one word it's the big よ and in the other, it's the small よ.

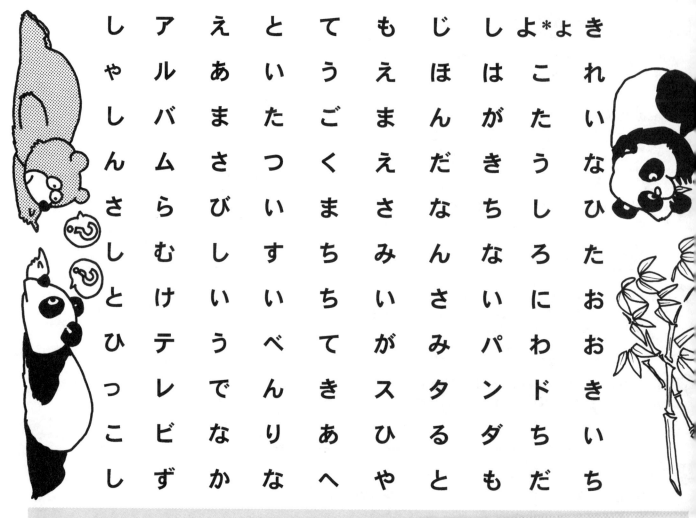

```
し　ア　え　と　て　も　じ　し　よ　＊よ　き
ゃ　ル　あ　い　う　え　ほ　は　こ　　　れ
し　バ　ま　た　ご　ま　ん　が　た　　　い
ん　ム　さ　つ　く　え　だ　き　う　　　な
さ　ら　び　い　ま　さ　な　ち　し　ろ　ひ
し　む　し　す　ち　み　ん　な　ろ　に　た
と　け　い　い　ち　い　さ　い　に　わ　お
ひ　テ　う　べ　て　が　み　パ　わ　ド　お
っ　レ　で　ん　き　ス　ン　ン　ド　ち　き
こ　ビ　な　り　あ　ひ　タ　ち　い　だ　い
し　ず　か　な　へ　や　と　も　だ　ち
```

again（また）	box	desk lamp	house	how	room
album	chair	dictionary	in front of	on/above	small
bear	clock/watch	duck	inside	panda（パンダ）	spacious
behind	cold	English	letter	photo	town/city
beside	comics	everyone	lonely/sad（さびしい）	postcard	TV
big	convenient	friend	lots/many	pretty/clean	under
bookcase	desk	garden	moving	quiet	very

Message: _____, which is what Yuki has!

There have been some changes to Hiroshi's room. Study the *before* and *after* pictures and complete the sentences to describe the differences in the position of the items (*hint:* write your sentences according to the *after* picture).

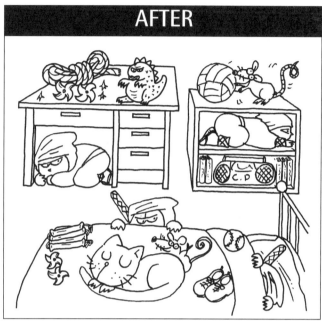

a　<u>ベッドの　うしろに　にんじゃが　います。しろが　いません。</u>

b　

c　

d　

e　

f　

g　

h　

おべんとう　クイズ

1 Circle the correct answer.

a If someone asked you へやに　ベッドが
ありますか which would be the best answer
according to the picture?

- はい、います。
✓ • はい、あります。
- いいえ、いません。
- いいえ、ありません。

b If someone said to you はこは　どこに
ありますか s/he would be asking:
✓ • where is the box?
- what is in the box?
- who is in the box?

c If someone asked you どんな　ぬいぐるみでか,
which two answers would be correct?
✓ • かわいい　ぬいぐるみです。
- えみこさんの　ぬいぐるみです。
✓ • きれいな　ぬいぐるみです。

d The most appropriate way to start a letter to
Chieko is:
- ちえこさん　より。
✓ • ちえこさんへ。
- ちえこさんです。

e The most appropriate answer to the question
ゆきさんは　どこに　いますか is:
✓ • トイレに　います。
- トイレに　あります。
- テレビの　中に　います。

f Ninja were famous for their skills in:
- flower arranging.
- building.
✓ • espionage/spying.

2 Match the phrases with the most appropriate
situation where you might use them.

B **a** もう、うるさい！　　A when you want to
see someone again

A **b** また、あいたいです。 B when you've had
~~want~~ 　　enough of being
annoyed

C **c** あそびに　　　　　C when you want
きてください。　　someone to come
to visit

D **d** ほら！　　　　　　D when you want to
alert someone to
look at something

3 Complete the adjectives in these sentences by
adding い or な as required.

a あたらし（い）ほんです。

b ひろ（い）へやです。

c べんり　な　うちです。

d すてき　な　アパートです。

e かわい（い）ねこです。

f しずか　な　にわです。

4 Answer the following questions about your own room

a へやに　ベッドが　ありますか。
はい、あります。

b ベッドの　よこに　つくえが　ありますか。
　　　　　beside　　desk
はい、＿＿＿＿＿＿＿＿＿＿＿＿＿＿＿＿＿
(go to question c)

いいえ、＿＿＿＿＿＿＿＿＿＿＿＿＿＿＿
(go to question d)

c つくえの　上に　本が　ありますか。
＿＿＿＿＿＿＿＿＿＿＿＿＿＿＿＿＿＿＿＿
(go to question e)

d つくえは　どこに　ありますか。
＿＿＿＿＿＿＿＿＿＿＿＿＿＿＿＿＿＿＿＿
(go to question e)

e どんな　へやですか。
＿＿＿＿＿＿＿＿＿＿＿＿＿＿＿＿＿＿＿＿

unit 4
あちこち！

1

Listen to the recording and tick the correct location.

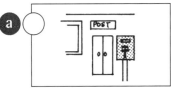 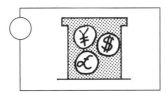 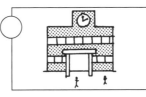 

c  こうべえき  きょうとえき 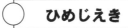 ひめじえき  ひろしまえき

d 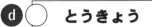 とうきょう 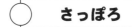 さっぽろ  ふじさん  こうべ

e 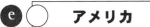 アメリカ  オーストラリア  カナダ  日本

2

Listen to the recording and tick the correct destination.

 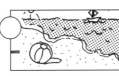 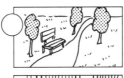 

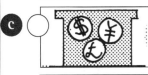   

3

Listen to the recording and circle the correct information for each place mentioned in the conversation.

a

八時から　十時まで
九時から　十一時まで
九時から　二時まで
九時から　一時まで

b

月曜日から　金曜日まで
火曜日から　金曜日まで
火曜日から　日曜日まで
水曜日から　木曜日まで

c

六時から　十時まで
六時から　十一時まで
六時半から　十一時まで
六時から　十時半まで

d

カーニバル

十時から　四時まで
十二時から　五時半まで
十二時半から　五時まで
二時から　五時半まで

4

Part A

In pairs, make up a dialogue using the school calendar below. Your host sister or brother is asking you about your school work, assignment due dates and social life. Answer his/her questions according to the information in the calendar. This task may be assessed by your teacher.

BLM Extra 8 (Speaking assessment sheet) Ask your teacher for the assessment criteria.

五月

月	火	水	木	金	土	日
	1	2	しんじと 3 かいもの（プレゼント）	4	5 パーティー	6 テニス
7	8	すうがくの 9 しゅくだい	10	日本ごの 11 しゅくだい	12 テニス	13
14 （ちえこさんと えいが）	15 スポーツデー	16	えいごの 17 しゅくだい	かいもの 18	としょかん 19 インターネット	20
れきしの 21 しゅくだい	22	ちりの 23 えんそく	24	25	26	27 テニス
28	29	30	かがくの 31 しゅくだい			

しゅくだい
しゅくだい
しゅくだい

Part B

Now, use your own diary and talk about your schedule with your friends.

5

Look at the pictures below and complete the sentences
using から and まで as appropriate.

a

d

b

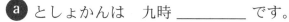

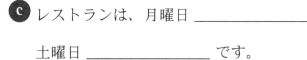

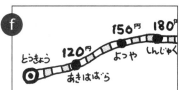

a としょかんは　九時 _____ です。

b スーパーは _____ からです。

c レストランは、月曜日 _____

土曜日 _____ です。

d ジャズショーは _____ です。

e せんせいは _____ ひまです。

f _____ 150えんです。

6

Answer the questions in Japanese, referring to each picture.

a

デパートの　セールは　いつから　いつまでですか。

_____

b

このしんかんせんは　どこまで　行きますか。

_____

c

このみせは　何時から　何時まで　**あいていますか。**

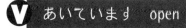

_____

d

どこまでですか。

_____

e

すみません、マドンナの　コンサートは　いつから　いつまでですか。

_____

On the recording you will be asked a question about each item. Answer in the negative. You do not need to write down your answers.

a All the questions use い adjectives.

b The following questions all use な adjectives. Remember the rules are different to the い adjectives!

8

Complete the sentences using an appropriate adverb.

a いぬは ＿＿＿＿＿＿＿＿＿＿＿＿ かわいいです。 （とても／あんまり）

b トラックは ＿＿＿＿＿＿＿＿＿＿ はやくないです。 （とても／ぜんぜん）

c かばんは ＿＿＿＿＿＿＿＿＿＿ おもいです。 （あんまり／ちょっと）

d じてんしゃは ＿＿＿＿＿＿＿＿ あたらしくないです。 （ちょっと／あんまり）

9

Survey at least five of your friends to complete the survey sheet.

a 日本ごは　おもしろいですか。

b ～さんの　がっこうは
あたらしいですか。

c カンティーンの　サンドイッチは
たかいですか。

d 日本ごの　クラスは　しずか
ですか。

e 日本ごが　すきですか。

f うちから　がっこうまで
とおいですか。

	とても	すこし／ちょっと	あんまり	ぜんぜん
a				
b				
c				
d				
e				
f				

10

Change the following sentences into the negative. As you work through the list, write the English meanings.

い adjectives

a おかしいです。	おかしくないです。	*It is not funny.*
b おもいです。		
c はやいです。		
d たかいです。		
e おそいです。		
f あたらしいです。		
g ちいさいです。		

な adjectives

a	ゆうめいです。	ゆうめいじゃないです。	*It is not famous.*
b	でんとうてきです。		
c	だいじょうぶです。		
d	じょうずです。		
e	べんりです。		
f	すてきです。		
g	だいすきです。		

11

Using the English clues, complete the sentences in Japanese.

a はやい_____ バスです。 It's a fast bus.

b _____ でんしゃです。 It's a slow train.

c _____ タワーです。 It's a tall★ tower.

d _____ つくえです。 It's a heavy desk.

e _____ デパートです。 It's a convenient department store.

f _____ かたなです。 It's an interesting samurai sword.

g _____ おしろです。 It's a famous castle.

h _____ たてものです。 It's a traditional building.

i _____ きっぷです。 It's an expensive★ ticket.

Tall and expensive are the same word in Japanese.

12

Part A

Complete these sentences using the English word in brackets and then give the English for each sentence.

a こうえんは ＿＿とおいです。＿＿ (far away) ＿＿＿ *The park is far away.* ＿＿＿

b くるまは ＿＿＿＿＿＿です。 (fast) ＿＿＿＿＿＿＿＿＿＿＿＿＿

c 日本ごが ＿＿＿＿＿＿です。 (I'm good at) ＿＿＿＿＿＿＿＿＿＿＿＿

d トム・クルーズは ＿＿＿＿＿です。 (famous) ＿＿＿＿＿＿＿＿＿＿＿＿＿

e たてものは ＿＿＿＿＿＿です。 (tall) ＿＿＿＿＿＿＿＿＿＿＿＿＿

f はこは ＿＿＿＿＿＿です。 (heavy) ＿＿＿＿＿＿＿＿＿＿＿＿＿

g おしろは ＿＿＿＿＿＿です。 (traditional) ＿＿＿＿＿＿＿＿＿＿＿

h けしきは ＿＿＿＿＿＿です。 (pretty) ＿＿＿＿＿＿＿＿＿＿＿＿＿

Part B

Rewrite the sentences from **Part A** in the negative.

Remember when a な adjective comes before です, な is not required.

a こうえんは とおくないです。

とおくない！

b
c
d
e
f
g
h

Rank the following pictures by ticking the most appropriate description. Compare your results with a partner. Do they differ?

たてものは

○ とても　でんとうてきです。
○ ちょっと　でんとうてきです。
○ あんまり　でんとうてきじゃないです
○ ぜんぜん　でんとうてきじゃないです

けしきは

○ とても　きれいです。
○ ちょっと　きれいです。
○ あんまり　きれいじゃないです。
○ ぜんぜん　きれいじゃないです。

テニスが

○ とても　じょうずです。
○ ちょっと　じょうずです。
○ あんまり　じょうずじゃないです。
○ ぜんぜん　じょうずじゃないです。

しんかんせんは

○ とても　はやいです。
○ ちょっと　はやいです。
○ あんまり　はやくないです。
○ ぜんぜん　はやくないです。

スニーカーは

○ とても　たかいです。
○ ちょっと　たかいです。
○ あんまり　たかくないです。
○ ぜんぜん　たかくないです。

Read the following entry from Yuki's diary and answer the questions in English.

八月六日　月曜日　はれ

今日、神戸から　さっぽろに　ひっこしを　した。①
あさ　十時に　神戸を　出た。② そして、ごご　四時に
あたらしい　うちに　ついた。③ まだ、あたらしい
うちは　すきじゃない。私と　私の　かぞくは
ひこうきで　さっぽろまで　きた。④ ベッドや　つくえや
ソファーなどは　トラックで　はこんだ。⑤ うちの
ちかくに　ショッピングセンターが　ある。⑥ あした
あさから、おかあさんと　いっしょに　かいものを
する。⑦

Japanese people don't always finish off their sentences using です or ます. As this is a diary entry, there's no need to be too polite. This list shows the plain form and the equivalent polite form of the verbs. The meaning for each verb is the same.

① した　　　　しました
② でた　　　　でました
③ ついた　　　つきました　*arrived*
④ きた　　　　きました
⑤ はこんだ　　はこびました
　　　　　　　transport, carry
⑥ ある　　　　あります
⑦ する　　　　します

a Give the English for the katakana words.

1 ベッド _____

2 ソファー _____

3 トラック _____

4 ショッピングセンター _____

What does the passage say about the ショッピングセンター?

(i) _____

(ii) _____

b What happened to Yuki at these times?

1 あさ　十時 _____

2 ごご　四時 _____

c Two types of transport are mentioned. Write each type below and explain what each was used for.

_____

_____

Before you listen to the recording, study the place names on the map of Japan. As you listen, number the city where each person lives.

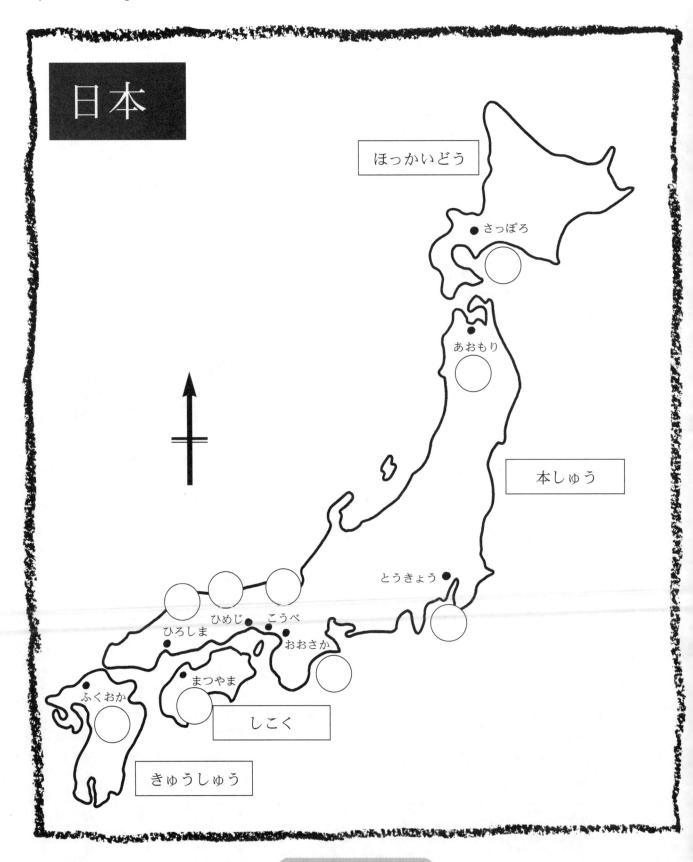

日本

ほっかいどう

さっぽろ

あおもり

本しゅう

とうきょう

ひめじ

こうべ

ひろしま

おおさか

まつやま

ふくおか

しこく

きゅうしゅう

Part A

Before you listen to the recording, study the map. Then, as you listen, draw an arrow from where each person lives to where each person went.

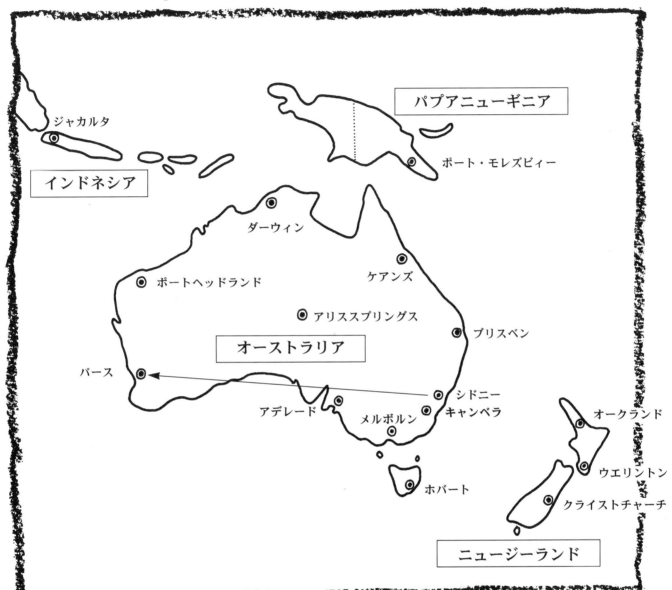

Part B

Listen to the recording again and write down in English the mode of transport.

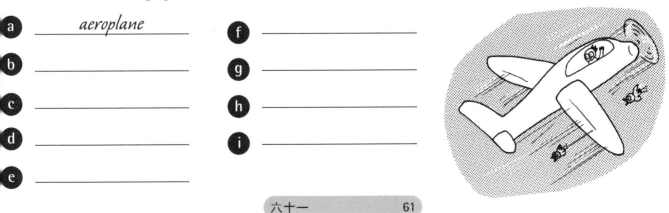

a *aeroplane*

b

c

d

e

f

g

h

i

17

Part A

Answer the questions in Japanese in your exercise book.

a おじいさん／おばあさんは　どこに　すんでいますか。
どのぐらい　すんでいますか。

b おじさん／おばさんは　どこに　すんでいますか。
どのぐらい　すんでいますか。

c あなたは　どこに　すんでいますか。
どのぐらい　すんでいますか。

Part B

BLM 4.1 (Jigsaw) Ask your teacher for the game instructions.

18

Read the newspaper article about Mr Kinoshita and answer the
questions in English.

①あった　　あいまし〜
②だ　　　　です
③いる　　　います
④かいしゃ
⑤ゆうめいだ　*company*
⑥ある　　　ゆうめいで
　　　　　　あります
⑦一時間
⑧かかる　　*for one hour*
⑨のうじょう　かかります
　　　　　farm

木下　きんたろう

今日、まちで　おもしろい　人に　**あった**。名前は　木下さん**だ**。
　　　　　　　　　　　　　　　　　　　①

木下さんは　三十二さいで、さっぽろに　四年ぐらい
②

すんで**いる**。くるまの　セールスマン**だ**。
　　　③

木下さんの　**かいしゃ**は　おおきくない。でも、さっぽろで
　　　　　　④

ゆうめいだ。木下さんの　かいしゃは　さっぽろえきの
⑤

ちかくに　**ある**。でも、木下さんの　うちは　かいしゃから
　　　　⑥

ちょっと　とおい。うちから　かいしゃまで　**一時間**ぐらい
　　　　　　　　　　　　　　　　　　　⑦

かかる。木下さんの　うちは　しずかで　ひろい　**のうじょう**の
⑧　　　　　　　　　　　　　　　　　　　　　⑨

中に　**ある**。

a Complete the following information about 木下さん in English.

Character: _____ Age: _____

Home: _____ Occupation: _____

木下さん's company: _____

b Complete the table.

Kanji	Kanji reading	English
な前	なまえ	
三十二さい		
四年ぐらい		
中に		

19

Use the English clues to write the following sentences in Japanese in your exercise book.

a I live in Japan. I've been living here for fourteen years.

b I live in Greece. I've been living here for one and a half years.

c I live in an apartment. I've been living here since January.

d I live near a river. I've been living here for five and a half years.

e I've been living above the flower shop for about three years.

f I've been living with my host sister since March.

20

Part A

In Japanese, write down the names of the school subjects in your exercise book:

a you are studying this year/semester.　　**b** you studied in Year 7.

Part B

Answer the following questions in Japanese.

a すきな　かもくは　何ですか。

_____

b きらいな　かもくは　何ですか。

_____

c 水曜日の　二時かんめは　何ですか。

_____

d 日本ごは　むずかしいですか。

_____

V 二時かんめ period two

Find the Japanese equivalent for the following words in the wordsearch below. Search for the words either from left to right or top to bottom. The remaining characters spell out a message.

かみひえおしろゆうめいしゃないですあしお
らぎすきですめうたじきぐらいじんきりずも
にねんさむらいびいきますちょっとたがかい
たきでんしゃえんいけしきすまちうなとでで
てっいここですきくまょごみだかていうすす
もぷまょいっしょにでうじまひくきましたか
のうすあたらしくないですせだにでぎんこう
だいじょうぶですとてもべんりですにくるま

a little	it's traditional
about	left
bank	let's go
building	near
car	physical education
castle	picture
dirty	post office
excuse me	right
famous	samurai
five o'clock	scenery
from	station
I came	thanks
I go	ticket
I like it	that's all right
I live	together
is it heavy?	train
it's convenient	two years
it's here	until
it's not	very
it's not new	yet
it's quiet	

IS IT HEAVY?

Complete this sentence with the remaining characters to find out where Ben and Takako went.

ベンくんと　たかこさんは ＿＿＿＿＿＿＿＿＿＿＿＿＿＿＿＿＿行きました。

Pretend to be your favourite movie star or musician. Sanae is conducting an interview with you. Complete the conversation in Japanese by filling in the speech bubbles. When you have finished, practise with your classmates. For those of you who are Sanae, before you begin, check the pronunciation of the star's name with your teacher.

おべんとう　クイズ

1 Match the English and Japanese:

はやく　　　　　　　　that's all right
むかし　　　　　　　　picture
だいじょうぶです　　　hurry up!
おしろ　　　　　　　　medieval Japanese warrior
もってください　　　　please hold it
けしき　　　　　　　　long ago
さむらい　　　　　　　castle
え　　　　　　　　　　scenery

2 How would you answer in Japanese if someone asked you these questions:

a どこに　すんでいますか。
_____

b どのぐらい　すんでいますか。
_____

3 Circle the correct particle.

a ひめじじょう（が、か、の）すきです。
b でんしゃ（に、は、で）はやいです。
c おしろ（に、か、は）でんとうてきです。
d 日本ご（で、と、が）じょうずですか。
e きっぷ（の、は、で）たかいですね。

4 Use the words from the list to make appropriate answers to the questions.

十二時　　　　　九時　　　　　トロント
一時半　　　　　三月　　　　　金曜日
九月　　　　　　月曜日　　　　メルボルン

a どこから　ですか。
_____

b いつまで　ですか。
_____

c 何時まで　ですか。
_____

d いつから　ですか。
_____

e どこまで　ですか。
_____

f いつから　いつまで　ですか。
_____

g 何時から　何時まで　ですか。
_____

5 Answer the questions in the negative.

a あたらしいですか。（No it's not new.）
_____

b きれいですか。
_____

c しずかですか。
_____

d むずかしいですか。
_____

e たてものは　おおきいですか。
_____

f こうえんは　ゆうめいですか。
_____

g きっぷは　たかいですか。
_____

6 Answer the questions using the hints given.

a おそいですか。(a little)
_____

b むずかしいですか。(not really)
_____

c きたないですか。(not at all)
_____

d ゆうめいですか。(quite)
_____

e しずかですか。(very)
_____

f でんとうてきですか。(not at all)
_____

g いいですか。(very)
_____

h べんりですか。(not really)
_____

7 Make up an appropriate answer to each of the questions about this train.

この　でんしゃは
a どこからですか。

_____

b どこまでですか。

_____

8 Answer the following questions using the hints given.
a デパートは　どこですか。

_____
(near the station)

b トイレは　どこですか。

_____
(near the exit)

c ちえこさんは　どこに　すんでいますか。

_____
(near Kobe)

d えみこさんは　どこに　すんでいますか。

_____
(in Hakata)

e ともだちは　どこに　すんでいますか。

_____
(near the park)

f ゴジラは　どこに　すんでいますか。

_____
(near the sea/beach)

g ブラッドピットは　どこに　すんでいますか。

_____
(in America)

9 Answer the following sentences truthfully in Japanese.
a すうがくが　すきですか。

_____

b 日本ごが　すきですか。

_____

c たいいくが　じょうずですか。

_____

d れきしが　きらいですか。

_____

e コンピューターが　すきですか。

_____

f へびが　きらいですか。

_____

10 Pick out the odd word in each group and explain your choice.
a きっぷ　　こうえん　　おしろ　　たてもの
b ええー　　なあ　　　ええと　　あのう
c どんな　　どこ　　　いつ　　　おなじ
d おしろ　　かたな　　えき　　　さむらい

11 Complete these sentences using the English hints given.
a _____ ゆうめい_____ 。
(It's very famous.)

b _____ たか_____ 。
(It's not expensive at all.)

c _____ あたらしい_____
(It's quite new.)

d _____ べんり_____ 。
(It's not really convenient.)

12 How would you thank someone in each of the following situations?
a You're a shop assistant thanking a customer when they leave.

_____

b Thanking your friend for moving over to allow you to sit down.

_____

c Thanking a senior student for saying that they will find a book for you.

_____

13 Read the following sentences aloud.
a くるまで　行きました。
b えきの　前からです。
c でんしゃは　とても　はやいです。
d デパートは　ぎんこうの　右に　あります。
e 何時からですか。
f ベンくんの　左に　すわりました。
g 五年ぐらい　ジャカルタに　すんでいます。

unit 5

きせつ

1

Look at the diagrams provided. Before you listen to the recording, study the position of the books in relation to the people. As you listen, tick the box of the most appropriate location.

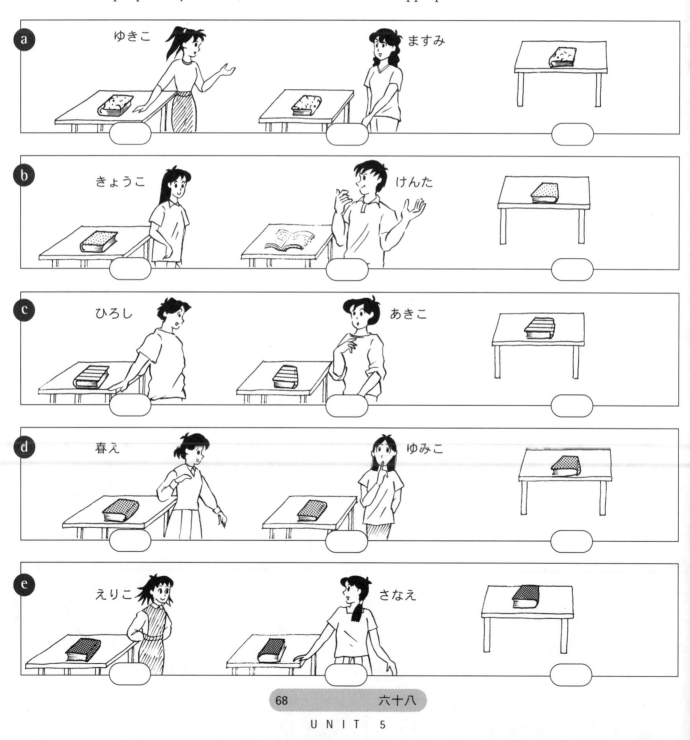

2

BLM 5.1 (ピーナツ　ゲーム) Ask your teacher for the game instructions.

3

Match the Japanese and English sentences by placing the appropriate number beside the Japanese sentence.

a ◯ あのくるまは　せんせいのですか。　　**1** This car was expensive.

b ◯ このくるまは　せんせいのですか。　　**2** Is that car over there the teacher's?

c ◯ そのくるまは　あたらしいですか。　　**3** Is that car new?

d ◯ そのくるまは　たかかったです。　　　**4** Is that car over there new?

e ◯ このくるまは　たかかったです。　　　**5** Is this car the teacher's?

f ◯ あのくるまは　あたらしいですか。　　**6** That car was expensive.

4

Part A

Study the position of the objects in relation to the people in the picture. With a partner, pretend you are the people in the picture and take it in turns to ask who owns the following items (〜は　だれのですか). Then write your sentences on the next page. Check your answers with your classmates.

Part B

When asking who owns the item, you will need to consider whether この、その or あの is used. The following example may help you.（ゆきこ）テニスラケット（Yukiko must speak about the tennis racket.）ゆきこ says このテニスラケットは　だれのですか。
(Yukiko uses この because she is near the tennis racquet.)

a （ちえこ）本 その本は　だれのですか。_____

b （けんいち）本 _____

c （さなえ）テニスラケット _____

d （けんいち）バレーボール _____

e （ゆきこ）ふでばこ _____

f （さなえ）ケーキ _____

g （ゆきこ）コーヒー _____

h （けんいち）コーヒー _____

i （ちえこ）ケーキ _____

j （ゆきこ）バスケットボール _____

5

Listen to the following short passages and fill in the sentences in English.

a Kenta's favourite _____ is _____ because he loves _____ and _____ are fun.

b Mariko's _____ day is _____ because she _____ and does _____ . After that she has _____

c Masumi's _____ television programs are _____ . She watches them everyday from _____ to _____ . Last year her favourite cartoon was Astro Boy but this year she likes _____ .

d John thinks Titan is the _____ attraction but, Free fall is the _____ John suggests _____ on _____ .

e Emiko went to the zoo _____ . She saw lions which were the _____ animals. She thought the monkeys were _____ , but the _____ were the _____ .

6

Conduct this survey around your class and record the answers you are given.

a　いちばん　すきな　きせつは　何ですか。<u>ジョンくんの　いちばん　すきな　きせつは　春です。</u>

b　いちばん　きらいな　かもくは　何ですか。_____

c　いちばん　やさしい　かもくは　何ですか。_____

d　いちばん　むずかしい　スポーツは　何ですか。_____

e　いちばん　いそがしい　日は　何曜日ですか。_____

f　いちばん　すきな　まんがは　何ですか。_____

g　いちばん　すばらしい　えいがは　何ですか。_____

h　いちばん　はやい　でんしゃは　何ですか。_____

i　いちばん　いい　ともだちは　だれですか。_____

7

Complete the sentences by writing your answers in Japanese. For *n* and *o*, write your own sentences. First, study the way the sentences are formed:

でんしゃ　*train*
たかい　でんしゃ　*expensive train*
いちばん　たかい　でんしゃ　*most expensive train*
いちばん　たかい　でんしゃは　〜でしょう　*the most expensive train is probably ...*

a　日本で　いちばん　たかい　でんしゃは　_____でしょう。

b　日本で　いちばん　はやい　でんしゃは　_____でしょう。

c　日本で　いちばん　おおきい　まちは　_____でしょう。

d　いちばん　ゆうめいな　日本の　たべものは　_____でしょう。

e　いちばん　ゆうめいな　日本の　はなは　_____でしょう。

f　いちばん　でんとうてきな　日本の　スポーツは　_____でしょう。

g　日本で　いちばん　さむい　きせつは　_____でしょう。

h　日本で　いちばん　あつい　きせつは　_____でしょう。

i　日本の　こどもの　いちばん　たのしい日は　_____でしょう。

j 日本で　いちばん　すばらしい　まつりは ＿＿＿＿＿＿＿＿＿＿＿＿＿＿でしょう。

k ＿＿＿＿＿＿＿＿＿＿＿＿＿＿＿＿＿＿＿は　すうがくでしょう。

l ＿＿＿＿＿＿＿＿＿＿＿＿＿＿＿＿＿＿＿は　テニスでしょう。

m ＿＿＿＿＿＿＿＿＿＿＿＿＿＿は　チョコレートでしょう。

n ＿＿＿＿＿＿＿＿＿＿＿＿＿＿＿＿＿＿＿＿＿＿＿＿＿

o ＿＿＿＿＿＿＿＿＿＿＿＿＿＿＿＿＿＿＿＿＿＿＿＿＿

8

Answer the questions in Japanese.

a いちばん　すきな　おかしは　何ですか。 ＿＿＿＿＿＿＿＿

b テレビで　いちばん　おもしろい　ばんぐみは　何ですか。 ＿＿＿＿

c がっこうで　いちばん　むずかしい　かもくは　何ですか。 ＿＿＿＿

d いちばん　すきな　スポーツは　何ですか。 ＿＿＿＿＿＿＿＿＿

e 日本ごの　クラスで　いちばん　げんきな　人は　だれですか。 ＿＿＿

f テレビで　いちばん　おもしろい　まんがは　何ですか。 ＿＿＿＿＿

g いちばん　すきな　うたは　何ですか。 ＿＿＿＿＿＿＿＿＿＿＿

h どうぶつえんで　いちばん　おおきい　どうぶつは　何ですか。 ＿＿＿

9

Make up your own sentences using the word given in the brackets, to say something is *the most . . .*

> Study how to form the sentences:
> まんがは　*Barbie World*　です。
> つまらない　まんがは　*Barbie World*　です。
> いちばん　つまらない　まんがは　*Barbie World*　です。

a （つまらない）いちばん　つまらない　まんがは　*Barbie World*です。

b （たかい） ＿＿＿＿＿＿＿＿＿＿＿＿＿＿＿＿＿＿＿＿＿＿＿

c （いい） ＿＿＿＿＿＿＿＿＿＿＿＿＿＿＿＿＿＿＿＿＿＿＿＿

d （おいしい） ＿＿＿＿＿＿＿＿＿＿＿＿＿＿＿＿＿＿＿＿＿＿

e （むずかしい） ＿＿＿＿＿＿＿＿＿＿＿＿＿＿＿＿＿＿＿＿＿

f （いそがしい） ＿＿＿＿＿＿＿＿＿＿＿＿＿＿＿＿＿＿＿＿＿

g （すてきな） ＿＿＿＿＿＿＿＿＿＿＿＿＿＿＿＿＿＿＿＿＿＿

h （ゆうめいな） ＿＿＿＿＿＿＿＿＿＿＿＿＿＿＿＿＿＿＿＿＿

i （しずかな） ＿＿＿＿＿＿＿＿＿＿＿＿＿＿＿＿＿＿＿＿＿＿

10

Before you listen to the recording, read the reasons below. As you listen to the questions, select an appropriate answer from the reasons given. Insert the letter in the space provided.

Reasons

1 たかかったから。   3 あついから。   5 むずかしいから。

2 おもしろくないから。   4 あつくないから。   6 まずいから。

ⓐ ◯   **ⓑ** ◯   **ⓒ** ◯   **ⓓ** ◯   **ⓔ** ◯   **ⓕ** ◯

11

Before you listen to the recording, read the questions below. As you listen to the reasons given, choose an appropriate question. Follow the same procedure as in the previous task.

Questions

1 なぜ　夏休みが　すきですか。   4 なぜ　やきそばを　つくりましたか。

2 なぜ　そのまんがを　かいましたか。   5 なぜ　このみずが　きらいですか

3 なぜ　あのどうぶつが　こわかったですか。   6 なぜ　まちに　あるいて　行きませんか。

ⓐ ◯   **ⓑ** ◯   **ⓒ** ◯   **ⓓ** ◯   **ⓔ** ◯   **ⓕ** ◯

12

Think of five people in your class (including your teacher!) to whom you would like to ask a question. For example, you may want to ask why your teacher likes Japanese: せんせい、なぜ　日本ごが　すきですか. First write your questions and then ask your classmates and teacher. Write their answers. You should ask questions to at least five different people.

Questions	Answers
a	
b	
c	
d	
e	

13

Match the reasons to the questions. Write the appropriate number beside each question.

ⓐ なぜ　冬が　すきですか。 ⑤ **1** やすかったから。

ⓑ なぜ　パーティーに　行きませんか。 ◯ **2** あつくないから。

ⓒ なぜ　きょう　およぎませんか。 ◯ **3** おもしろかったから。

ⓓ なぜ　このケーキを　たべませんでしたか。 ◯ **4** つまらないから。

ⓔ なぜ　ディスコに　行きませんか。 ◯ **5** スキーが　おもしろいから。

ⓕ なぜ　ふでばこを　かいませんでしたか。 ◯ **6** たかかったから。

ⓖ なぜ　きのう　カラオケで　うたいませんでしたか。 ◯ **7** まずかったから。

ⓗ なぜ　そのテレビの　ばんぐみを　みましたか。 ◯ **8** はずかしかったから。

ⓘ なぜ　あの　CDを　かいましたか。 ◯ **9** いそがしいから。

ⓙ なぜ　うちで　べんきょうしませんか。 ◯ **10** うるさいから。

14

Using the information in the pictures, answer the questions in Japanese.

なぜ　この本を　よみましたか。

_____

なぜ　そのテストが　すきでしたか。

_____

なぜ　きょう　およぎますか。

_____

なぜ　あのえいがを　みませんでしたか。

_____

なぜ　木曜日が　きらいですか。

_____

なぜ　かきごおりが　すきですか。

_____

15

Study the activities in the pictures before you listen to the recording. Number the activities as you hear them.

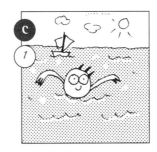

16

Listen to the dialogues and answer the questions in English.

a **1** What time did the person get up today? _____

2 What did he do today? _____

3 Who is Akira? _____

4 What plans do they have? _____

b
1 When was this person's birthday? _____
2 How did she celebrate it? _____
3 What was disappointing? _____
4 What did she enjoy about it? _____

c
1 What did Kenta ask Toshio? Where was it? _____
2 What did Toshio think of it? _____
3 What were they looking at together? _____
4 Who are they talking about? _____
5 What did Toshio do there? _____

d
1 What does Emiko offer Karen? _____
2 How does Karen respond and why? _____
3 What Japanese food does Karen like best? _____
4 What is Karen disappointed about? _____

17 👥

BLM 5.2 (Connect and collect!) Ask your teacher for the game instructions.

18

Read the list of activities and allocate them to the most appropriate season by writing the letter in the season bubble.

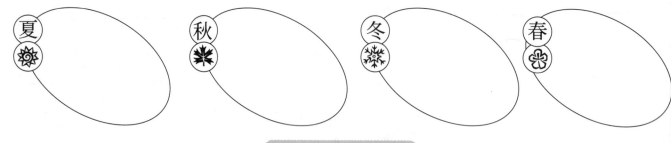

a	はなみに　行きます。	**i**	うみに　あそびに　行きます。
b	水じょうスキーに　行きます。	**j**	じょうばを　します。
c	おつきみを　します。	**k**	おんせんに　行きます。
d	しゅうがくりょこうに　行きます。	**l**	バーベキューを　します。
e	ゆきだるまを　つくります。	**m**	やまのぼりを　します。
f	おもちを　たべます。	**n**	年がじょうを　かきます。
g	やまに　ドライブに　行きます。	**o**	おとしだまを　もらいます。
h	りょこうを　します。	**p**	やきいもを　たべます。

19

Read the passages for each season and note in point form as much information as you can in your exercise book.

春

いちばん　すきな　きせつは　何ですか。わたしは　春が　すきです。
さむい　冬の　あと、春の　まいにちは　たのしいです。
ともだちと　こうえんに　あそびに　行きます。ひなまつりは　三月です。
ことし　わたしの　おかあさんは　すてきな　ひなにんぎょうを
かいました。ひなにんぎょうは　たかかったです。それから、四月に
かぞくと　はなみの　ピックニックを　します。きれいな　さくらの
はなを　みに　行きます。ときどき　春に　りょこうを　します。
きょねん　おかあさんと　おとうさんと　おんせんに　行きました。
あつい　おんせんで　リラックスしました。とても　よかったです。

夏

あついから　ぼくは　夏が　だいすきです。ぼくの　うちは　うみから
とおくないから、よく　うみに　サーフィンに　行きます。ときどき
ともだちと　水じょうスキーを　しに　行きます。ボートが　はやいから
とても　たのしいです。よる、こうえんで　バーベキューを　します。
それから、はなびを　みます。ぼくの　まちの　はなびは　とても
すばらしいです。あつい　日に　かきごおりを　たべます。おいしいです。
ぼくの　がっこうの　夏休みは　七月十五日から　八月三十一日までです。
いちばん　ながい　休みです。夏は　いいですね。

秋は 九月から 十一月までです。夏は とても あついから
ちょっと きらいです。でも 秋は あつくないから とても
いいです。らいしゅうの 土曜日は わたしの がっこうの
ぶんかさいです。ともだちと がっこうに あそびに
行きます。コンサートや ゲームや おいしい たべものが
たくさん あります。わたしも ともだちも この日が
だいすきです。それから、秋は まつりが たくさん
あります。いちばん おもしろい まつりは おつきみです。
おつきみの 日は うちで パーティーを します。みんな
きれいな つきを みに きます。それから、やきいもを
たべます。とても おいしいです。わたしの おじいさんは
ときどき 秋の はいくを つくります。はいくは
むずかしいから おもしろいです。ことしの 秋、
しゅうがくりょこうに 行きました。ひろしまの

へいわこうえん peace park

へいわこうえんに 行きました。**へいわこうえんは** ちょっと
こわかったです。でも、しゅうがくりょこうは とても
たのしいですよ。

わたしの いちばん たのしい きせつは 冬です。きょねん
ともだちと ゆきだるまを たくさん つくりました。
さむかったから、こうえんに ジョギングに 行きませんでした。
十二月の さむい 日に うちの 中で 年がじょうを
かきました。十二月三十一日に おとうさんと おもちを
つくりました。一月一日から 三日までは おしょうがつです。
おしょうがつは だいすきです。おとしだまを もらいます。
いいですよ。いそがしかったから きょねんの 冬は スキーに
行きませんでした。でも、ことしの 冬は ともだちの かぞくと
スキーに 行きます。

Using each picture as a guide, in pairs, write a few lines in Japanese in your exercise books. This can be a narrative, (a passage about the picture) a recount, (re-telling the story about the picture) or a dialogue between two or more people about the picture. You could also use the picture as a basis for a cartoon-type script.

21

Translate the following sentences into Japanese.

a Let's go to the beach for a swim. _____

b Why didn't you like that movie? _____

c We like sushi because it is delicious. _____

d **A:** Where are my shoes? _____

B: They are under the chair. _____

e **A:** Who is that person over there? _____

B: It is Shingo. _____

f Which book do you like best? _____

g **A:** Which band do you like best? _____

B: I like ～ best because they are fantastic. _____

Seasons board game

From スタート, work your way one square at a time to the New Year's celebrations at the bottom right square. **Do not move diagonally**. To be able to move on the next turn, you must identify the correct season in Japanese for the activity or festival in the square you are on. If you give the season **and** exact date for the squares marked ✳ you can move two squares.

One player:

Count the number of squares it takes you to finish, adding one point for each square you couldn't get. Try a different path and see which gives you the lowest score.

Two or more players:

Take it in turns to move. If your answer is incorrect, you miss a turn. The first person to finish wins.

おつきみを します。		ひなまつり です！	水じょう スキーを します。	やまのぼりを します。
おんせんに はいります。	年がじょうを かきます。	はなびを みに 行きます。		おとしだまを もらいます。
うんどうかい です。				こうようは すばらしい です。
秋まつりです。 やきいもを たべます。	うみで およぎます。	みなさん あけまして おめでとう！✳	オーストラリア デーです！	ぶんかさい です！
おはなみを します。		おもちを たべます。	たなばた です！	さくらの はなを さきます。
五月 にんぎょうです！✳				おせちりょうりを たべます。
やまで スキーを します。	スノーボードを します。	どくりつさいです。✳ （アメリカの インデペンデントデー）	うみに サーフィンに 行きます。	木の 下で ピクニックを します。

しんねん おめでとうございます。

ことしも よろしく おねがいします。

おべんとう　クイズ

1　Circle the correct answer.

  a　When you want to tell someone that you took **this** photo you would say:
- あのしゃしんを　とりました。
- このしゃしんを　とりました。
- そのしゃしんを　とりました。

  b　If someone asked you いちばん　さむい きせつは　いつですか, you would answer:
- 秋です。
- 春です。
- 冬です。
- 夏です。

  c　If someone asks you なぜ　夏が すきですか s/he would be asking:
- do you like summer?
- do you like summer best?
- why do you like summer?

  d　If someone asks you そのまんがを よみましたか, s/he is talking about:
- the comic in your hand.
- the comic in his/her hand.
- the comic the teacher is holding.

  e　When someone says きもちが　いい, s/he is saying:
- s/he feels good.
- s/he feels bad.
- s/he is looking forward to something.

2　Circle the odd word in each row.

さんぽ	およぎ	やま
こうよう	かどまつ	おつきみ
すばらしい	たのしい	きれい

3　Fill in the blank spaces with appropriate words.

  a　やまに ＿＿＿＿＿＿＿ に　行きます。

  b　なぜ　スノーボードを　しますか。

    ＿＿＿＿＿＿＿ から。

  c　いちばん　おいしい　おかしは

    ＿＿＿＿＿＿＿ です。

  d　ともだちと ＿＿＿＿＿＿＿ に

    ＿＿＿＿＿＿＿ に　行きます。

4　Match the phrases by writing the number of the English beside its Japanese equivalent.

  a（　）しゅうがくりょこうに　行きました。

  b（　）おんせんに　はいりました。

  c（　）たのしみね。

  d（　）ことしも　よろしく　おねがいします。

  e（　）さくらは　おきなわから

    ほっかいどうまで　さきます。

  f（　）いっしょに　ピクニックを

    しませんか。

  g（　）ぼくは　つりが　だいすきです。

  h（　）たのしかったから。

  i（　）いぬと　こうえんに　行きました。

1　I'm looking forward to it.
2　Do you want to go on a picnic together?
3　I went on a school trip.
4　I went to the park with the dog.
5　Be my friend this year too.
6　I love fishing.
7　I went into a hot spring.
8　Because it was fun.
9　The cherry blossoms bloom from Okinawa to Hokkaido.

5　Answer the questions in Japanese.

  a　いちばん　すきな　スポーツは 何ですか。

    ＿＿＿＿＿＿＿＿＿＿＿＿＿＿＿＿

  b　夏休みに　何を　しますか。

    ＿＿＿＿＿＿＿＿＿＿＿＿＿＿＿＿

  c　いちばん　おもしろい　えいがは 何ですか。

    ＿＿＿＿＿＿＿＿＿＿＿＿＿＿＿＿

  d　いつ　おせちりょうりを　たべますか。

    ＿＿＿＿＿＿＿＿＿＿＿＿＿＿＿＿

1

From the list below, write the Japanese equivalent for each weather logo.

雨、 はれ、 くもり、 かぜが つよい、 雪、 ふぶき、 あらし、 たいふう

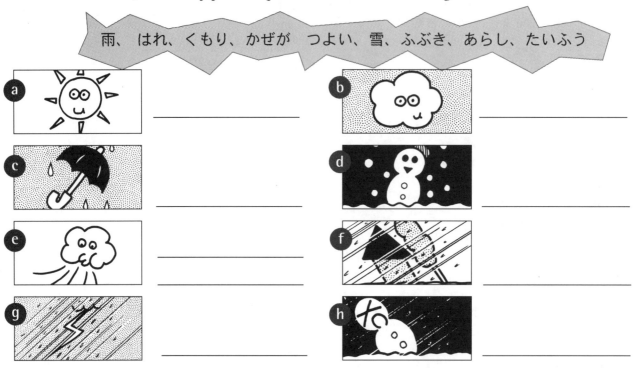

a _____

b _____

c _____

d _____

e _____

f _____

g _____

h _____

2

Listen to the recording and complete the table using the Japanese weather descriptions from Task 1.
Note that some days have more than one description.

	きのう	きょう		こんや
a		(i)		
		(ii)		
b		(i)		
		(ii)		
c	(i)			
	(ii)			

3

BLM 6.1 (天気は　どうですか) Ask your teacher for the instructions.

4

Read だいすけ's account of his camping trip and answer the questions in English.

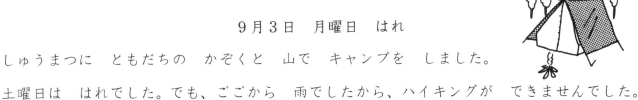

9月3日　月曜日　はれ

しゅうまつに　ともだちの　かぞくと　山で　キャンプを　しました。
土曜日は　はれでした。でも、ごごから　雨でしたから、ハイキングが　できませんでした。
テントの　中で　ゲームを　しました。それから、こわい　はなしも　ききました。
ちょっと　こわかったです。日曜日も　雨　ときどき　くもりでした。かぜが
つよかったから、ハイキングに　行きませんでした。また、テントの　中で　カラオケを
しました。ぼくの　ともだちの　おとうさんは　うたが　とても　へたです。へんな
キャンプでした。でも、とても　たのしかったです。

When was the account written and what was the weather like on that day?

a 1 Date: _____

   2 Day of the week: _____

   3 Weather: _____

b What did Daisuke say about the weather on each day?

   1 Saturday: _____

   2 Sunday: _____

c What did Daisuke do on each day?

   1 Saturday: _____

   2 Sunday: _____

5

Read the dialogue and answer the questions in English.

りょうた： もしもし、まりさん、ぼく、りょうたです。ぼくの　おとうさんが　あたらしい　ボートを　かいましたよ。

まり： へえ、ボートを　かいましたか。すごいですね。

りょうた： きょう、かぞくと　ビーチに　行きます。まりさんも　行きませんか。

まり： えっ？ビーチ？ビーチは　ちょっと...きょうは　雪ですよ。

a Tick the correct alternative.

The conversation is taking place:

· at school.

· at the beach.

· on the telephone.

· at the shop.

b Who bought the boat?

_____

What did Ryota ask Mari?

_____

c What was Mari's response? Why?

_____

6

Using だいすけ's account in Task 4 as a guide, write an account in your exercise book of what you did yesterday and today. Your account should begin with the dates, days of the week and the weather. Include what activities you did and how you enjoyed them.

7

Part A

Before you listen to the weather report on the recording, read the weather descriptions and the city names.

 はれ

 雨

 くもり

 かぜが　つよい

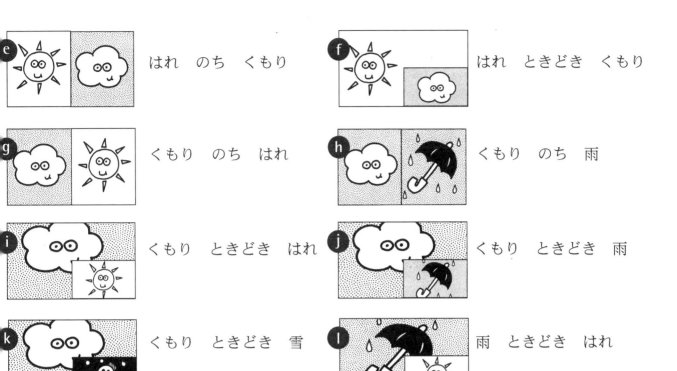

e はれ　のち　くもり　　　f はれ　ときどき　くもり

g くもり　のち　はれ　　　h くもり　のち　雨

i くもり　ときどき　はれ　　j くもり　ときどき　雨

k くもり　ときどき　雪　　　l 雨　ときどき　はれ

Part B

As you listen, complete the table by writing the letter of the appropriate weather logo for each city.
Note there are two descriptions for Tokyo's weather.

	16日	17日	18日
さっぽろ			
せんだい			
とうきょう			
にいがた			
なごや			
おおさか			
ひろしま			
たかまつ			
ふくおか			
おきなわ			

きょうは　16日です。

8

You are a weather reporter giving today's weather forecast (1 6 日). Read aloud the information in Task 7 to give the weather broadcast for at least six of the cities. Your partner will give you a score out of ten for accuracy and fluency. Practise three times.

1st attempt
Score: _____ /10

2nd attempt
Score: _____ /10

3rd attempt
Score: _____ /10

9

Read the following passages and fill in the appropriate weather logos in the weather chart on the following page.

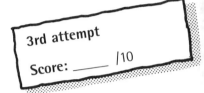

２月２４日　金曜日の　天気よほうです。

さっぽろの　きょうの　天気は　くもり　のち　雪でしょう。あしたは
くもり　ときどき　雪でしょう。２６日は　雪でしょう。

せんだいの　きょうの　天気は　くもりでしょう。あしたは　はれ
のち　くもりでしょう。２６日は　はれ　ときどき　くもりでしょう。

とうきょうの　きょうの　天気は　くもりでしょう。あしたは　くもり
ときどき　雨でしょう。２６日は　はれ　ときどき　くもりでしょう。

にいがたでは　雨　のち　雪でしょう。それから、あしたと
２６日は　くもり　ときどき　雪でしょう。

なごやの　きょうの　天気は　くもりでしょう。あしたは　くもり
のち　はれでしょう。２６日は　はれ　ときどき　くもりでしょう。

おおさかは　きょうは　くもり　ときどき　雨でしょう。あしたは
雨でしょう。２６日の　天気は　くもり　のち　はれでしょう。

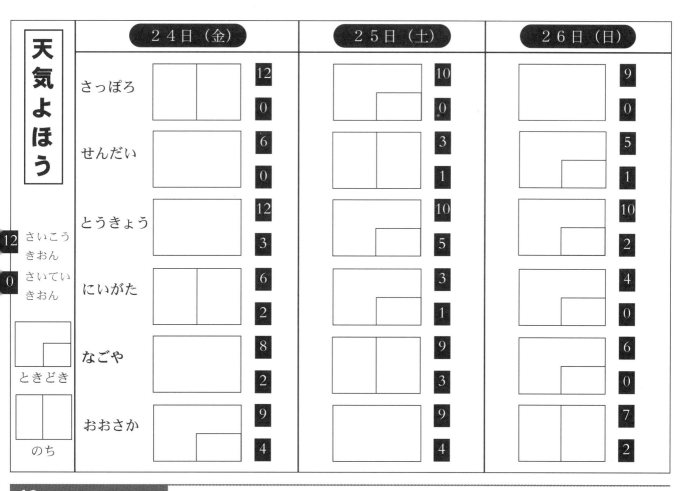

10

Using the weather chart, write a weather report for the following cities.

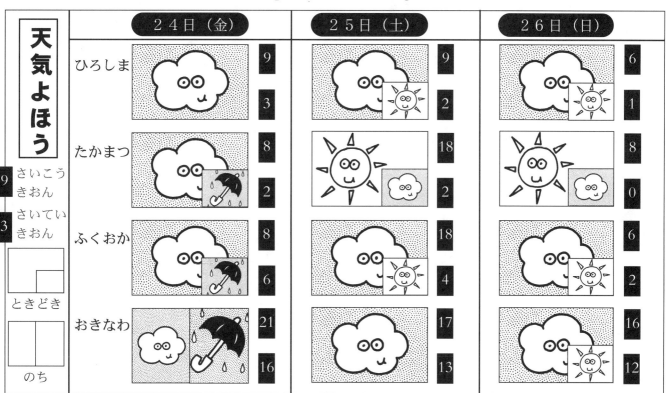

a ひろしま _____

b たかまつ _____

c ふくおか _____

d おきなわ _____

11 🔍 📖

Before you listen to the recording, read the weather descriptions and the city names. As you listen to the world weather report, write the letter of the appropriate weather description and temperature for each city.

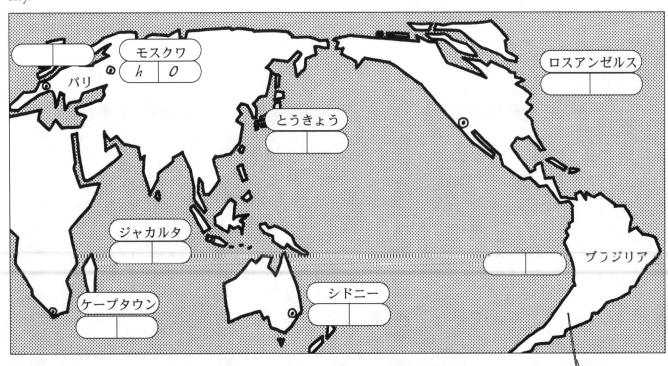

a はれ

b はれですが、あさから かぜが つよい

c 雪 のち 雨

d くもり のち はれ

e くもり のち 雨

f はれ ときどき 雨

g はれ ときどき くもり

h はれ のち くもり

12

Listen to the recording to fill in the temperature on the thermometers and what was said about the temperature in Japanese (e.g. さむい、あたたかい).

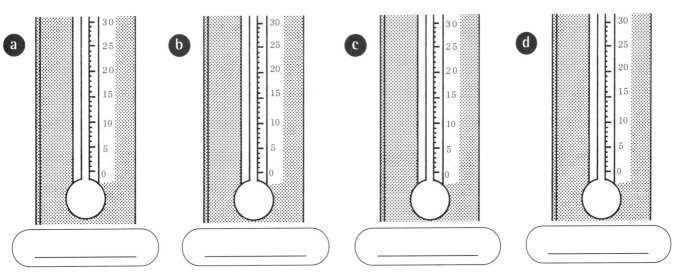

a   b   c   d

13

Listen to the recorded weather forecast and fill in the highest and lowest temperatures for each city in English.

City	Highest	Lowest
a Tokyo		
b Nagoya		
c Osaka		

14

Ask your partner temperature of the three cities from Task 13. S/he will answer by giving the highest and lowest temperatures. The following example may help you.

Q: とうきょうの　きおんは　何どですか。

A: さいこう　きおんは　〜ど、さいてい　きおんは　〜どです。

One point is awarded for each correct highest and lowest temperature. Write your partner's score. Then swap roles.

Your score

Score: _____ /6

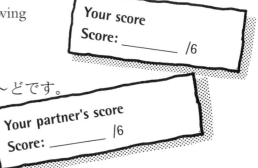

Your partner's score

Score: _____ /6

15

BLM 6.2 (きおんは　何ど？) Ask your teacher for the instructions.

たか子 and ちえ子 are deciding on activities for the kendo camp. Look at the weather chart from the newspaper and fill in the missing parts of the conversation with an appropriate word or the temperature.

ちえ子：	たか子さん、キャンプは　24日から　27日までですね。
	24日は ＿＿＿＿＿＿＿ ですよ。ジョギングが　できますね。
たか子：	いいえ、キャンプは　27日の　月曜日から　29日の　水曜日までです。
	27日は ＿＿＿＿＿ です。さいこう　きおんは ＿＿＿＿＿
	ど、　さいてい　きおんは ＿＿＿＿＿＿ どです。さむいから、
	ジョギングを　して、ウォーミングアップを　しましょう。
	それから、そとで　サーキットトレーニングを　しましょう。
ちえ子：	そうですね。そのあと、けんどうの　れんしゅうを　します。
	28日の　天気は ＿＿＿＿＿＿ です。
	さいこう　きおんは ＿＿＿＿＿＿ ど、さいてい　きおんは
	＿＿＿＿＿＿ どです。一日あたたかいですね。
たか子：	28日は　ちかくの　スポーツセンターに　行きませんか。
	ウォーミングアップに　すいえいを　しましょう。そのあと、エアロビクスを
	しましょう。それから、けんどうの　れんしゅうを　します。
ちえ子：	はい。29日の　天気は　どうですか。
たか子：	29日の　天気は ＿＿＿＿＿＿ です。さいこう　きおんは
	＿＿＿＿＿＿ ど、さいてい　きおんは ＿＿＿＿＿＿ どです。
	いやですね。ジムで　ウエイトトレーニングを　しませんか。
ちえ子：	そうですね。それから、ミーティングを　しましょう。
	きょねんの　しあいの　ビデオを　みます。ミーティングの　あとで
	けんどうの　れんしゅうを　しましょう。

Listen to the conversation and number the pictures in the order you hear them.

18

BLM 6.3 (Sugoroku game) Ask your teacher for the game instructions.

19

In Japan, people make wishes by writing them on an えま board and hanging them in shrines. It is interesting to read the wishes. Read the following えま boards and answer the questions in English.

とうきょうだいがくに はいりたいです。
こうこう三年 おか みち子

ピアノを じょうずに ひきたいです。
いしの まゆみ 10さい

V じょうずに　very well

MBMの バスケットボールの せんしゅに なりたいです。
西高校 バスケットボールクラブ
たかだ まさお

ふじい　たけしくんの
ガールフレンドに
なりたい。
中学2年
あさの　とも子

アメリカに　行きたい。それから、
レオナルド・ディカプリオに
あいたいです。
みしま　ゆかり　２２さい

すうがくの　テストで
クラスで　いちばんに
なりたい。
はまぐち　よしのり

a Who wants to be a professional basketball player?

_____

b Who wants to get the best score in class? In what subject?

_____

c Who wants to be accepted to go to Tokyo University?

_____

d What is Mayumi's wish?

_____

e What does Yukari hope to do?

_____

20

Write your wish on the えま board.

Part A

Here is a typical Japanese letter to a friend. Read it and answer the questions in English.

ジェニーさんへ、

おげん気ですか。わたしは　げん気です。

日本は　いま　夏です。まいにち　あついから、がっこうの　プールで　およいでいます。きょうも　とても　いい天気です。さいこう　きおんは　３２どです。オーストラリアは冬ですね。オーストラリアの　冬は　雪が　ふりますか。

日本では　７月１６日から　８月３１日まで　夏休みです。休みには　かぞくと　アメリカをりょこうします。わたしと　おとうさんは　ディズニーランドに　行きたいです。でも、おとうとは　ハリウッドに　行きたいです。おかあさんは　ラスベガスに　行きたいです。いそがしいですね！ジェニーさんの　がっこうにも　七月に　休みが　ありますか。休みに何を　したいですか。

らい年は　オーストラリアを　りょこうしたいです。

じゃあ、また　てがみを　かいてください。さようなら。

７月２日

いしだ　まり　より

a Divide the letter into six sections: addressee, letter opening, main passages, letter ending, date and sender.

b Who is the letter from and to? _____

c When was it written? _____

d What did the writer say about the weather in Japan?

1 season: _____

2 weather: _____

3 temperature: _____

e List three things the writer and her family want to do in America.

1 _____

2 _____

3 _____

Part B

Using the letter as a guide, in your exercise book, write Jenny's response to Mari in Japanese.

First, write the Japanese equivalents for the English words and then search for them in the puzzle. All words can be found by searching horizontally or vertically. The characters are used once! Unjumble the remaining eleven characters to reveal the hidden message!

あ	か	ぜ	が	つ	よ	い	と
た	も	さ	だ	ち	と	で	か
た	さ	い	こ	う	き	お	ん
か	す	て	と	し	ょ	か	ん
い	け	い	や	な	て	ん	き
ふ	ぶ	き	え	た	い	ふ	う
す	た	お	い	い	ね	ぁ	り
ず	せ	ん	ぷ	う	き	ら	ょ
し	む	し	あ	っ	い	し	う
い	あ	め	の	ち	く	も	り
は	れ	と	き	ど	き	ゆ	き

a. warm _____

b. cool _____

c. humid _____

d. blizzard_____

e. stormy _____

f. typhoon _____

g. windy _____

h. highest temperature _____

i. lowest temperature _____

j. awful weather _____

k. rain later cloudy _____

l. sunny with some snow_____

m. fan_____

n. swimming (search diagonally!) _____

o. cooking_____

p. library _____

Hidden message! ____ ____ ____ ____ ____ ____ ____ ____ ____ ____ ____ !

おべんとう クイズ

1 Circle the most appropriate answer.

a If someone said こんやの 天気は
  どうですか, s/he is asking:
  - what was the dinner like tonight?
  - how are you tonight?
  - what is the weather like tonight?

b いやな 天気です means:
  - it is nice weather.
  - it is awful weather.
  - it is bad weather.

c If the weather was stormy yesterday, you
  would say:
  - きのうは あらしでした。
  - きのうは ふぶきでした。
  - きのうは たいふうでした。

d If today's weather is expected to be cloudy and
  then rain,you would say:
  - きょうは くもり ときどき 雨です。
  - きょうは 雨 のち くもりです。
  - きょうは くもり のち 雨です。

e If yesterday's lowest temperature was two degrees
  and the highest temperature was fourteen degrees,
  and you were asked きのうの さいこう
  きおんは 何どでしたか, you would reply:
  - 二どでした。
  - 十四どでした。
  - 二どから 十四どでした。

f If it is humid today, you would say:
  - きょうは あついです。
  - きょうは むしあついです。
  - きょうは あたたかいです。

g きょう 何を したいですか, means:
  - what are you doing today?
  - what is the weather like today?
  - what do you want to do today?

h ストーブを けしたくないです。でも、
  せんぷうきを つけたいです means:
  - the person wants to turn off the heater and
    turn on the fan.
  - the person doesn't want to turn off the heater
    but turn on the fan.
  - the person wants to turn on the heater and
    turn off the fan.

i The standard opening to Japanese folk tales is:
  - もしもし。
  - むかし むかし。
  - おかし おかし。

j Your mother says いってらっしゃい to you
  when you:
  - leave home.
  - return home.
  - telephone home.

k もうすぐ means:
  - very soon.
  - not for a long time.
  - wait a moment.

l If you need to scream for help, you would say:
  - げんき。
  - どうしよう？
  - たすけてー。

m ビュービュー is the sound effect for:
  - blowing wind.
  - singing birds.
  - heavy rain.

n えど was the old name for:
  - Japan
  - Tokyo
  - Kyoto

2 Match the Japanese and English words.

a あらし   sunny

b はれ   stormy

c 雨   a blizzard

d ふぶき   typhoon

e たいふう   cloudy

f くもり   rainy

g 雪   snowy

h あたたかい   cool

i さむい   humid

j すずしい   warm

k むしあつい   hot

l あつい   cold

3 Choose the correct particle.

a あした （で、に、の）　天気は　どうですか。

b エアコン （と、を、に）つけたいです。

c あさって、何 （の、と、を）したいですか。

d ごごから　かぜ （が、に、と）
つよいでしょう。

e テレビ （と、の、が）天気よほう （を、と、
に）みましたか。

4 Look at the weather chart and complete the
following sentences in Japanese.

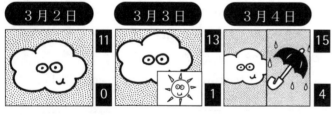

三月二日の　天気は ＿＿＿＿＿＿＿ です。

さいてい　きおんは ＿＿＿＿＿＿ です。

さむいですね。

三月三日の　天気は ＿＿＿＿＿＿＿ です。

さいこう　きおんは ＿＿＿＿＿＿＿です。

三月四日の　天気は ＿＿＿＿＿＿＿＿

です。さいこう　きおんは ＿＿＿＿＿＿＿、

さいてい　きおんは ＿＿＿＿＿＿＿です。

すずしいでしょう。

5 Part A

Read the New Year's wishes made by members of
Yumi's family and answer the questions in English.

一月一日
ストーブを　かいたいです。かぞくと
おんせんに　行きたいです。日曜日に
りょうりを　したくないです。
山中　春子　４２さい

一月一日
がっこうで　テストを　したくないです。
ともだちと　かっこいい　くるまで
ドライブしたいです。あたらしい
ディスクマンを　かいたいです。
山中　ゆうー　こうこう三年せい

a What are Yumi's brother's wishes?

＿＿＿＿＿＿＿＿＿＿＿＿＿＿＿＿＿＿＿＿

＿＿＿＿＿＿＿＿＿＿＿＿＿＿＿＿＿＿＿＿

b Who wants to go to the hot springs?

＿＿＿＿＿＿＿＿＿＿＿＿＿＿＿＿＿＿＿＿

Part B

Write your wish list in your exercise book in Japanese.

6 Answer the questions in Japanese.

a きょうの　天気は　どうですか。

b あついですね。およぎたいですか。

＿＿＿＿＿＿＿＿＿＿＿＿＿＿＿＿＿＿＿

c がっこうの　あとで　としょかんに
行きたいですか。

＿＿＿＿＿＿＿＿＿＿＿＿＿＿＿＿＿＿＿

d あした、何を　したいですか。

＿＿＿＿＿＿＿＿＿＿＿＿＿＿＿＿＿＿＿

かんぱい！

1

Hiroshi's mother is asking Masako what activities she can or can't do. Write (O) for activities she **can do** or write (X) for those **she can't**.

2

On the recording, Yoshio will ask you what activities you can do. Using the cues given on the recording, respond to him after each question. A pause will be given on the recording. The first one is given as an example.

3

BLM 7.1 (Verb chart) Ask your teacher for some hints for remembering verb groups.

4

BLM 7.2 (Living in Japan - survey) Ask your teacher for the survey.

5

The following text is part of a well known English children's story. There may be some words you do not know, but you should be able to guess what is happening in each scene. Remember that's what learning language is all about! In your exercise book, draw an appropriate picture for each scene.

Before you begin this task, ask your teacher for BLM 7.3 (Body parts).

あかずきんちゃん

a おばあちゃん、あなたの　めは　おおきいですね。
あなたが　よく　みえますよ。

b おばあちゃん、みみが　おおきいですね。
よく　きこえますよ。

c おばあちゃん、はなが　おおきいですね。
よく　においが　**かげます**よ。　　**V かげます** can smell

d おばあちゃん、くちが　おおきいですね。
ああああ！
あなたが　よく　たべられます。

6

Part A
Place a **D** next to the verbs which mean *I do* . . . and a **C** next to the verbs which have been changed to mean *I can do* . . .

いきます	D	かけます	C	行けます	C
よめます		たべます		でかけます	
たべられます		ひきます		します	
でかけられます		のれます		あえます	
みます		うたえます		とります	
ひけます		かえます		できます	
とれます		うたいます		のります	
あいます		よみます		かいます	

Part B

Complete the table to say you *can do* each of the following actions. Be careful of the rules for the different groups of verbs.

Group 1 Verbs

a	かな**を**　かきます	かなが　かけます
b	かいます	
c	行きます	
d	はなします	
e	本を　よみます	
f	おはしを　つかいます	
g	まいにち、ファンタを　のみます	

Group 2 Verbs

a	りんご**を**　たべます	りんごが　たべられます
b	みせます	
c	あげます	
d	かぞえます	
e	土曜日に　でかけます	
f	ドアを　しめます	
g	せんせいは　日本ごを　おしえます	

おしえます　*teach*

Group 3 Verbs (Irregular)

a	きます	こられます
b	テニスを　します	テニスが　できます
c	からてを　します	
d	日本に　きます	
e	電わを　します	
f	かんじの　れんしゅうを　します	

Part C

Write the English for the sentences you made in **Part B**:

Group 1　f ： _____

Group 2　e ： _____

Group 3　f ： _____

The table shows the activities which Emiko, Hideki, Maki and Katsuhisa can do (O) and which they can't (X). ① indicates their favourite interest. In your exercise book, write a brief profile in Japanese for two people. Write at least four sentences about the activities they can or can't do. Also mention their favourite interest （きょうみ）.

きょうみ	えみこ (女)	ひでき (男)	まき (女)	かつひさ (男)
バンジージャンプ	① 0	X	X	X
りょうり	0	① 0	X	X
さんぽ	0	0	0	0
ゴルフ	X	0	0	① 0
本を　よみます	0	0	0	0
テニス	X	X	0	X
くるまを　れんしゅうします	X	0	① 0	X
えを　かきます	X	X	0	X
ピンポン	X	0	X	0

8

Part A

Listen to the recording and write the order of the numbers for each set as you hear them. Read through the numbers before you listen to the recording.

a | 十九 | | 九十 | | 二十 | | 九十一 | |

b | 百五十 | | 二百五十 | | 五百十 | | 二百七十 | |

c | 千九百十一 | | 千七百七十 | | 千四百 | | 二千五百二 | |

d | 三千百二十 | | 六千二百四十 | | 五千七百九十一 | | 八千二百五十三 | |

e | 一万五千 | | 三万一千二十 | | 六万四百 | | 百二十一万 | |

Part B

Give the Arabic numerals for the **second number** you heard on the recording in each set.

a _____   **d** _____

b _____   **e** _____

c _____

9 🐻 📖

Listen to the conversation between Kayo and Kenta who are preparing for their Mum's birthday.

a Complete the information below.

1 Item: _____ Price (arabic numerals): _____ Price (kanji): _____

2 Item: _____ Price (arabic numerals): _____ Price (kanji): _____

b Work out the total cost of the two items in Japanese to complete the sentence:

ぜんぶで_____ 円です。

---

10 👥

In pairs, answer the following questions in Japanese using the picture clues.

a おちゃは　いくらですか。

<u>百五十円（ひゃくごじゅうえん）です。</u>

b  天ぷらは　いくらですか。

c さしみは　いくらですか。

d ピザは　いくらですか。

e ぎょうざは　いくらですか。

f  ビールは　いくらですか。

g チョコレートパフェは　いくらですか。

h すきやきは　いくらですか。

i こうちゃは　いくらですか。

First, complete the dialogue between Yuusuke and the
salesperson. Then practise reading it aloud with a
partner so that you know it by heart. Pay attention to
your pronunciation, intonation, fluency and presentation.
This may be assessed by your teacher. BLM Extra 9
(Speaking assessment sheet). Ask your teacher for the
 assessment criteria.

てんいん:　　いらっしゃいませ！

ゆうすけ:　　＿＿＿＿＿＿＿＿　は　いくらですか。

てんいん:　　＿＿＿＿＿＿＿＿　円です。

ゆうすけ:　　ええと、＿＿＿＿＿＿＿＿　は　いくらですか。

てんいん:　　ちいさい＿＿＿＿＿＿＿　は　＿＿＿＿＿＿＿＿　円です。それから、

　　　　　　　　おおきい＿＿＿＿＿＿＿　は＿＿＿＿＿＿＿＿　です。

ゆうすけ:　　そうですか。じゃあ、＿＿＿＿＿＿＿　を＿二つ＿　、

　　　　　　　　＿＿＿＿＿＿＿＿　を＿＿＿＿＿＿＿　ください。

てんいん:　　はい、かしこまりました。

Add up each price list and then
work out how you would say the
totals in Japanese. (Hint: write your
answer in kanji to help you
pronounce it correctly). Then
with a partner, check your
answers by reading them aloud.

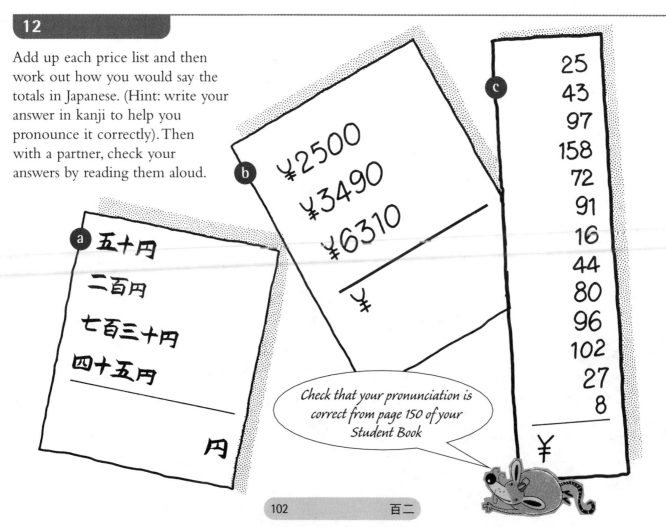

b
¥2500
¥3490
¥6310
¥

c
25
43
97
158
72
91
16
44
80
96
102
27
8
¥

a 五十円
二百円
七百三十円
四十五円
円

*Check that your pronunciation is
correct from page 150 of your
Student Book*

Part A

Choose five items from the menu on page 105 of your Student Book. Complete the table by finding out what the item is and briefly describing it in English. Note how much each one costs in yen and then work out how much this is in your currency.

Part B

Choose four items from the menu in your Student Book on page 105. In pairs, take it in turn to describe the cost of your chosen item. For example, you could say とりの　てりやきは 五百八十円です。 You do not need to write down your sentences.

たべもの	何？	¥	Your currency
a _____ _____			
b _____ _____			
c _____ _____			
d _____ _____			
e _____ _____			

Write these numbers in kanji. Follow the clues where given.

a 20500

$2 \times 10000 + 5 \times 100$

二万五百 _____

b 385

$3 \times 100 + 8 \times 10 + 5$

_____

c 4209

_____

d 75211

$7 \times 10000 + 5 \times 1000 + 2 \times 100 + 10 + 1$

_____

e 94866

_____

15 🐻 📼

Hisako and Hideki are planning a party. Write the number of each bottle of drink you hear mentioned in the conversation.

a	ファンタ	十二本
b	レモネード	
c	オレンジジュース	
d	サイダー	
e	コーラ	

16 🐻 📼

On the recording you will hear everyone arriving at a party. Everyone needs a drink before they can say かんぱい! Takahiro has found out what everyone wants and he is busy organising this with his Dad and sister. Before you listen to the recording, read through the types of drinks available. As you listen, record below how many of each type of drink is required. Then work out how many people are at the party.

a	コーヒー	三ばい
b	ビール	
c	ワイン	
d	こうちゃ	
e	水	
f	コーラ	
g	アップルジュース	

ぜんぶで　何人ですか。＿＿＿＿＿＿＿　です。

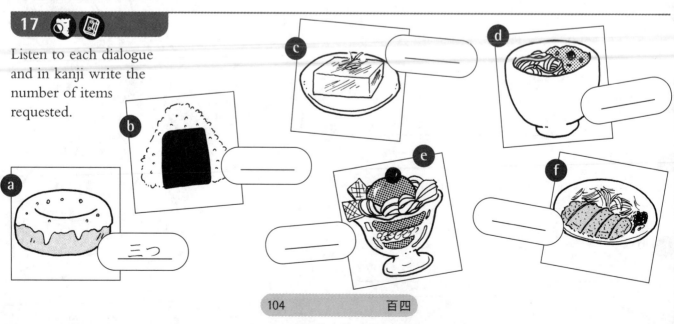

17 🐻 📼

Listen to each dialogue and in kanji write the number of items requested.

a 三つ

b

c

d

e

f

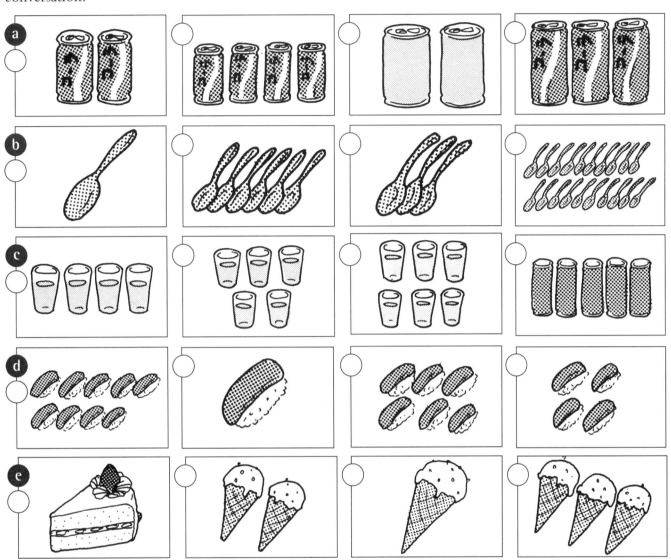

18

Listen to the recording and tick the picture which best indicates what is being ordered in each conversation.

a

b

c

d

e

19

Answer the questions about the following pictures in Japanese.

a　1　ビールは　何本ですか。

　　_____

　　2　ペンは　何本ですか。

　　_____

　　3　スプーンは　何本ですか。

　　_____

　　4　やきとりは　何本ですか。

　　_____

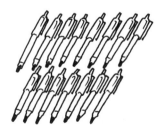

b

1 こうちゃは　何ばいですか。

＿＿＿＿＿＿＿＿＿＿＿＿＿＿＿

2 レモネードは　何ばいですか。

＿＿＿＿＿＿＿＿＿＿＿＿＿＿＿

3 おちゃは　何ばいですか。

＿＿＿＿＿＿＿＿＿＿＿＿＿＿＿

4 コーヒーは　何ばいですか。

＿＿＿＿＿＿＿＿＿＿＿＿＿＿＿

5 水は　何ばいですか。

＿＿＿＿＿＿＿＿＿＿＿＿＿＿＿

c

1 すしは　いくつですか。

＿＿＿＿＿＿＿＿＿＿＿＿＿＿＿

2 おにぎりは　いくつですか。

＿＿＿＿＿＿＿＿＿＿＿＿＿＿＿

3 ドーナツは　いくつですか。

＿＿＿＿＿＿＿＿＿＿＿＿＿＿＿

4 いすは　いくつですか。

＿＿＿＿＿＿＿＿＿＿＿＿＿＿＿

5 アイスクリームは　いくつですか。

＿＿＿＿＿＿＿＿＿＿＿＿＿＿＿

20

With a partner, in your notebooks, brainstorm a list in Japanese of all the objects which need the counters
〜本、〜はい、〜つ.You may need a dictionary or ask your teacher to find out other objects in
Japanese. See who can make the longest list! (Example: 〜本: バナナ、ビール、ペン、おはし ...)

21

Listen to the following conversation and tick the food items each person has decided to order.

	じろう	てるみ	たろう	なおみ
すきやき				
天ぷら				
カレーうどん				
ぎょうざ				
すし				
カリフォルニアロール				

Complete the last line with an appropriate sentence in Japanese.

a **てんいん:** いらっしゃいませ。
みち子: カップケーキは　いくらですか。
てんいん: カップケーキは　二百円です。_____

b **ひろみ:** すきやきを　ください。
ウェートレス: はい、_____

c **まさお:** 何に　しますか。
たかゆき: ピザに　します。きみは？
まさお: ぼくは　ハンバーグ_____

d **おかあさん:** エイミーさん、日本ごが　よめますか。
エイミー: はい、すこし　よめます。
おかあさん: かんじが　かけますか。
エイミー: いいえ、_____

23

Look at the menu on page 105 of your Student Book and decide on three dishes you would like to order. Then ask three people in your class what they will order and record their preferences below. You will be asked too!

わたし／ぼくは		と		と		に	します。

なまえ	何に			しますか。
a _____	_____	_____	_____	
b _____				します。
c _____	_____	_____	_____	

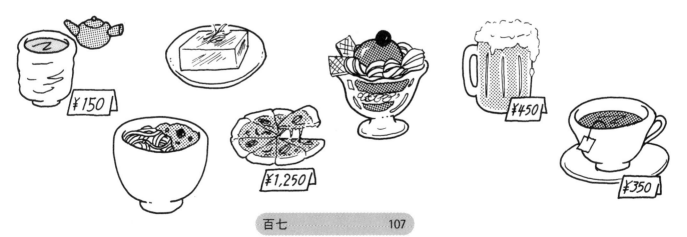

24

This is a conversation between 山本さん and a waiter. Number the statements in the correct order.

a ◯ それから、コーラと おちゃと 水を ください。

b ◯ はい、かしこまりました。

c ◯ はい、かしこまりました。

d ◯ 二本です。おちゃを 三ばいと 水を 二はい ください。

e ◯ 天ぷらを 二つと、カレーうどんを 四つと ハンバーグを 一つ ください。

f ◯ はい、コーラを 何本ですか。

25

Read the following dialogues and complete the missing food and quantities for the final order.

a

けい子:	ジュリーさん、何に しますか。
ジュリー:	わたしは やきとりと おにぎりに します。
けい子:	ウアンくん、何に しますか。
ウアン:	ぼくは カリフォルニアロールと 天ぷらに します。
けい子:	カレンさん、何に しますか。
カレン:	おにぎりと 天ぷらに します。
けい子:	わたしは やきとりと 天ぷらに します。すみません、_____ を _____ と、_____ を _____ と、_____ を _____ と、_____ を_____ ください。
ウェートレス:	はい、かしこまりました。

b

じゅん子:	のみものは ... えみ子さん、何に しますか。
えみ子:	ファンタに します。
しんご:	ぼくも ファンタに します。
まさ子:	わたしは おちゃに します。
じゅん子:	ケイトさん、トムくん、何に しますか。
ケイト:	ええと... ファンタに します。
トム:	コーラに します。
エリック:	ぼくも コーラに します。
カイリ:	オレンジジュースに します。
カーラ:	水と おちゃに します。じゅん子さんは？
じゅん子:	わたしも おちゃに します。すみません、
	_____
	_____
ウェーター:	はい、かしこまりました。

Shingo and his nine friends are eating at a restaurant. They have all given Shingo the exact money and asked Shingo to order for them. Complete the conversation using the prices from the menu on page 105 in the Student Book. Write the correct number of each item so that Shingo's total works exactly. *(Note: everyone is drinking juice).*

しんご: やきとりを ＿＿＿＿ と、とんかつを ＿＿＿＿ と、 天ぷらを ＿＿＿＿ と、わかめうどんを ＿＿＿＿ ください。ジュースも ください。

ウェートレス: ジュースを 何ばいですか。

しんご: ＿＿＿＿ ください。

ウェートレス: はい、かしこまりました。

八千九百八十円

At this restaurant the consumption tax has been included in the price.

Circle the odd one out.

a コーラ　ファンタ　レモネード　こうちゃ

b 百　千　万　円

c とんかつ　いつつ　ここのつ　みっつ

d しゃぶしゃぶ　よせなべ　天ぷら　すきやき

e 一本　日本　三本　何本

f いらっしゃいませ　いくらですか　かしこまりました　コーラを 何本ですか

g いただきます　ごちそうさま　かんぱい!　おなかペコペコ

h ビール　ジュース　こうちゃ　ビル

i コロッケ　スプーン　フォーク　おはし

Search the following words in Japanese. The words can be found horizontally from left to right or vertically from top to bottom. Some letters are used more than once. Complete the message below with the remaining characters.

た	べ	も	の	イ	お	は	し	か	ピ	ザ	お	り	ょ	う	り	ス	プ	ー	ン
ベ	ゲ	ッ	プ	タ	イ	ン	ド	し	コ	ー	ラ	レ	モ	ネ	ー	ド	お	そ	八
ら	お	な	こ	り	二	は	い	こ	の	五	本	い	に	お	ち	ゃ	な	ば	つ
れ	お	ま	う	ア	ビ	ー	ル	ま	み	は	や	く	九	つ	と	ん	か	つ	つ
ま	き	の	ち	五	や	二	う	り	も	ぎ	か	ら	ぎ	ょ	う	ざ	い	そ	か
す	い	さ	ゃ	千	き	百	ど	ま	の	さ	ん	で	あ	じ	ビ	ル	っ	れ	え
し	で	か	何	十	と	円	ん	し	り	む	ぱ	す	デ	ザ	ー	ト	ぱ	か	ま
水	す	な	本	一	り	あ	た	た	か	い	い	か	ジ	ュ	ー	ス	い	ら	す

Aji Building	drinks	India	quick
and then	eight things	It's big.	raw fish
beer	five (cylindrical objects)	Italy	spoon
burp	food	Japanese dim sims	sushi
cooking/cuisine	green tea	juice	two glasses
certainly	grilled chicken	lemonade	warm
Cheers!	How many (cylindrical) ?	nine things	water
chopsticks	How much is it?	noodles (buckwheat)	Western tea
cola	I can eat it.	noodles (wheat)	¥200
cold	I can use it.	pizza	5011
dessert	I'm full	pork cutlet	

Complete this sentence using the five remaining characters to show what Ben can make.

ベンくんは _____ が つくれます。

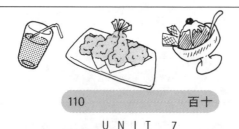

Truth or dare?
ほんとうの　ことを　いいましょうか。
ちょうせんに　おおじましょうか。

This game works best if played in pairs or a group. Choose ほんとうの　こと *(truth)* or ちょうせん *(dare)* each turn. If you can't *(or don't want to!)*, answer the question truthfully, or do the challenge you've picked, **you must follow the arrows to the opposite column and do what it says!**

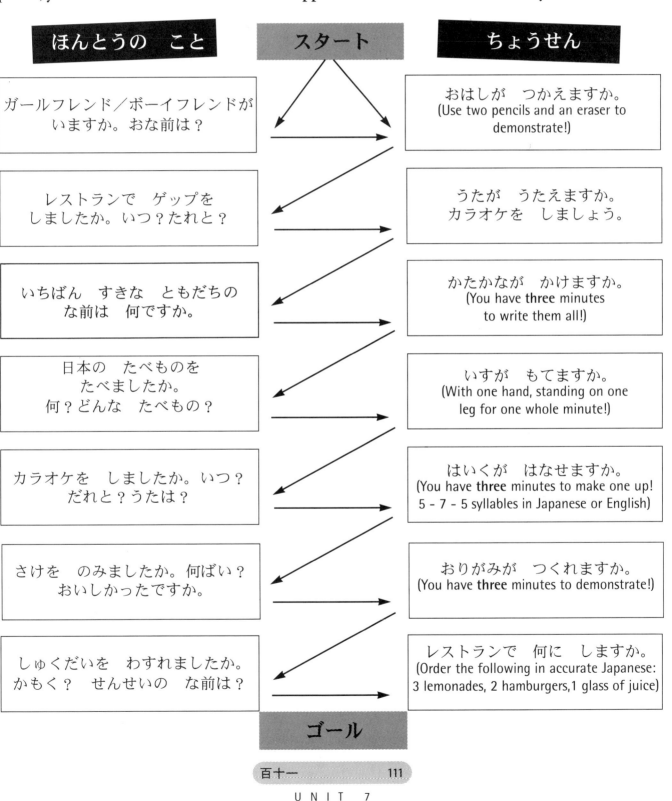

ほんとうの　こと	スタート	ちょうせん
ガールフレンド／ボーイフレンドが　います か。おな前は？		おはしが　つかえますか。 (Use two pencils and an eraser to demonstrate!)
レストランで　ゲップを　しましたか。いつ？たれと？		うたが　うたえますか。 カラオケを　しましょう。
いちばん　すきな　ともだちの　な前は　何ですか。		かたかなが　かけますか。 (You have **three** minutes to write them all!)
日本の　たべものを　たべましたか。何？どんな　たべもの？		いすが　もてますか。 (With one hand, standing on one leg for one whole minute!)
カラオケを　しましたか。いつ？だれと？うたは？		はいくが　はなせますか。 (You have **three** minutes to make one up! 5 - 7 - 5 syllables in Japanese or English)
さけを　のみましたか。何ばい？おいしかったですか。		おりがみが　つくれますか。 (You have **three** minutes to demonstrate!)
しゅくだいを　わすれましたか。かもく？　せんせいの　な前は？		レストランで　何に　しますか。 (Order the following in accurate Japanese: 3 lemonades, 2 hamburgers,1 glass of juice)

ゴール

おべんとう クイズ

1 Match the following vocabulary with its meaning as in the example.

イタリア	•	• warm
のみもの	•	• burp!
あたたかい	•	• Italy
デザート	•	• I'm starving!
ゲップ	•	• drinks
かんぱい	•	• I can use it
つかえます	•	• food
おなか　ペコペコ	•	• dessert
たべもの	•	• Cheers!

2 Circle the appropriate sentences a waiter or waitress could say to a customer in a restaurant.

a　はい、かしこまりました。
b　いくらですか。
c　おなか　いっぱい。
d　何本ですか。
e　いらっしゃいませ。
f　かんぱい！
g　ありがとうございました。

3 Number the foods according to the price tags from most expensive (1) to least expensive (4).

千二百円	二百八十円	三百九十円	八百円
_____	_____	_____	_____

4 Complete the sentences with the correct particle. Use は、が、に or を.

a　さしみ（_____）いくらですか。
b　おはし（_____）つかえます。
c　土曜日（_____）ピザ（_____）たべました。
d　水（_____）三ばいください。
e　らいねん、日本（_____）行けます。
f　すしと　天ぷら（_____）します。

5 Number the expressions in the order that you might logically say (or think) them at a mealtime.

①　おなか　ペコペコ
〇　ごちそうさま
〇　ゲップ
〇　おなか　いっぱい
〇　いただきます
〇　かんぱい！

6 Imagine you're at a Japanese restaurant. What would you answer if someone asked you
何に　しますか?

_____

7 Change these sentences to match the meaning given.
a　すきやきを　たべます。

_____
(I can eat sukiyaki.)

b　かんじを　かきます。

_____
(I can write kanji.)

c　サッカーを　します。

_____
(I can play soccer.)

d　ドアを　しめません。

_____
(I can't close the door.)

e　おはしを　つかいません。

_____
(I can't use chopsticks.)

f　日本の　しんぶんを　よみません。

_____
(I can't read the Japanese newspaper.)

g　パーティーに　いきません。

_____
(I can't go the party.)

8 Make up a question and answer in Japanese according to the pictures.

a

_____

_____

b

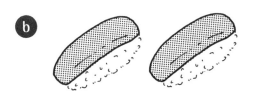

_____

_____

c

_____

_____

9 Say these numbers aloud in Japanese.

a	294	g	27381
b	638	h	56920
c	873	i	78103
d	1756	j	247196
e	4230	k	483011
f	8529	l	527985

10 Read aloud the following counters, paying attention to the correct pronunciation.

a 一つ、二つ、三つ、四つ、五つ、六つ、
七つ、八つ、九つ、十

b 一ぱい、二はい、三ばい、四はい、
五はい、六ぱい、七はい、八ぱい、
九はい、十ぱい

c 一本、二本、三本、四本、五本、六本、
七本、八本、九本、十本

11 You are wanting to find out how much something is or how many items there are. Write the letter of the question which is appropriate for the item.

a いくつですか。

b 何本ですか。

c 何ばいですか。

d いくらですか。

12 Answer the questions in Japanese.

a フランスごが　できますか。

_____

b さしみが　たべられますか。

_____

c 日本の　うたが　うたえますか。

_____

d テニスが　できますか。

_____

e おちゃが　のめますか。

_____

f かんじが　かけますか。

_____

unit 8

べんりな　フレーズブック

1

Listen to the recording and match the activity with the person by writing the appropriate letter.

2

Listen to Yuuji's speech about his host family and tick the correct photo of his family in each column.

Part A

This is a role-play between you as a receptionist at a child care centre (いくじしょ) and a family member. Every day, you receive telephone calls from a member of each child's family. Using the picture, respond by saying what their child or brother or sister is doing now. You receive four phone calls this day. The sample dialogue may help you.

You: もしもし、いくじしょです。

Caller: もしもし、けんたの　ははですが、けんたは　いま　何を　していますか。

You: けんたくんは　いま　本を　よんでいます。

はは	*mother*	ちち	*father*
あね	*older sister*	あに	*older brother*

These words are used when talking about yourself or your family to others.

Use おかあさん *etc. here because its not your Mum.*

Part B

You must keep a record of each telephone call. Complete the details in Japanese below.

	Child's name	Caller	Note
a	けんた	おかあさん	本を　よんでいます。
b			
c			
d			
e			

4

Link the English equivalents with the ます form and the て form for each verb.

a read •	• さわります •	• よんでいます •	• writing
b touch •	• かきます •	• さわっています •	• reading
c watch •	• よみます •	• べんきょうしています •	• touching
d study •	• かいます •	• 見ています •	• studying
e buy •	• べんきょうします •	• かっています •	• making
f write •	• 見ます •	• つくっています •	• watching
g make •	• つくります •	• かいています •	• buying

5

Read through the hints to find out which group the verb belongs to. Then write the verbs from the Verb Bank in the table below.

Group 1	Group 2	Group 3
These verbs end and an *i* sound before ます: ききます、はいります.	These verbs end with either an *e* or *i* sound before ます : たべます、見ます. The *i* ending verbs are often only one syllable: 見ます. Yet, be careful as there are some exceptions!	The only verbs in this group are きます, します and other combination verbs using します: べんきょうします.

Verb Bank

たべます	よみます	はいります	のります	ひっこしします	おしえます *to teach*
見ます	ねます *to sleep*	きます *to put on*	きます	あそびます	行きます
買います	しめます	うんてんします	見せます	かちます	あいます
つかいます					

Group 1	Group 2	Group 3

6

Change the verbs from the ます form into the て form. Write the English meanings for the て forms.

Group 1 Verbs	て form	English
すわります	すわっています	*I'm sitting*
買います		
はいります		
まちます		
よみます		
はなします		
さわります		
のみます		
かきます		
つくります		
Group 2 Verbs	**て form**	**English**
見ます	見ています	*I'm looking/watching*
たべます		
しめます		
見せます		
あけます		
Group 3 Verbs	**て form**	**English**
べんきょうします	べんきょうしています	*I'm studying*
します		
れんしゅうします		
電わします		
きます		

7

Make a set of twenty palm-sized flashcards using cardboard.

- On one side of each card, write the English for twenty verbs, on the other side of the card, write the **ます form** and the **て form** of the verb you have chosen.
- Colour code the border of each card: red for Group 1 verbs, blue for Group 2 verbs and yellow for Irregular verbs.
- Hole-punch one corner of the card and use a binder ring to hold the set together.
- Flip the cards and learn your verbs! As you come across new verbs, you can add to your collection.

8

Listen to the short conversation and number the pictures in the order you hear them. Then for each picture, place a (O) in the box if the person is **allowed** to do the activity or an (X) if s/he is **not allowed**.

a | 1 | 0

b

c

d

e

f

g

h

9

This task is a role-play for you and a partner for a conversation between you and your Japanese host brother or sister. Your host brother or sister has given you a note explaining the family routine.

However, you want to find out more details about the daily routine. For example, you might want to ask if you can use the telephone every week （まいしゅう 電わしても　いいですか）. Ask your host brother or sister six questions like this in Japanese.

七時に　おきます。
七時半に あさごはんを　たべます。
八時十五分に　がっこうに　行きます。
三時半に　がっこうから　かえります。
七時半に　ばんごはんを　たべます。
十時に　ねます。

Sometimes questions you might want to ask will be strange to a Japan *family. Discuss in class which questions are culturally appropriate a* *which ones seem inappropriate from a Japanese viewpoint.*

Role for host brother/sister

You are a host brother or sister. Complete the table using the questions you are asked. Decide on the answer from a Japanese family's viewpoint.

	Questions	Answer
a	*make phone calls every week*	*Yes*
b		
c		
d		
e		
f		
g		

10

BLM 8.1 (An ideal girlfriend/boyfriend!) Ask your teacher for the instructions.

11

Using the English meanings as clues, unjumble the sentences.

a あけても、を、まど、いいですか。 (May I open the window?)

_____

b に、あした、行って、パーティー、も、か、いいです。 (May I go to the party tomorrow?)

_____

c うんてんして、車、を、も、オートマチックの　いいですか。 (May I drive an automatic car?)

_____

d か、あなたの、いいです、つかって、も、を、じしょ。 (May I use your dictionary?)

_____

e か、かわ、およいで、と、も、ベンくん、いいです、で。 (May I swim at the river with Ben?)

_____

12

BLM 8.2 (What would you ask if ...?) Ask your teacher for the instructions.

13

Make up simple conversations for each of the situations below, by completing the bubbles. The pictures give you clues for when to use これ、それ or あれ.

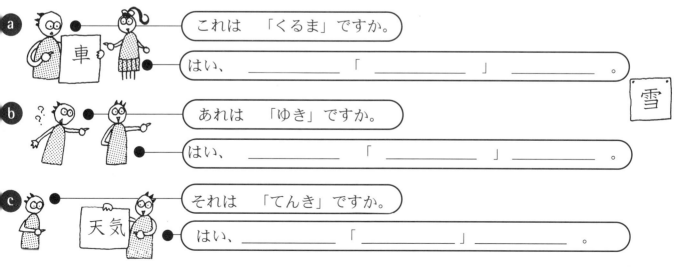

a これは　「くるま」ですか。

はい、_____　「_____」_____。

b あれは　「ゆき」ですか。

はい、_____　「_____」_____。

c それは　「てんき」ですか。

はい、_____　「_____」_____。

Part A

Before you begin this task, check that you have pencils or markers in the following colours: red, yellow, green, brown, grey, blue, orange and purple to colour in the items. If you don't have coloured pencils, write the colour of each picture underneath in English.

As you listen to the recording, colour, or write the colour of the items in each group according to the descriptions you hear.

Part B

Listen to the conversations between Akiko and Hiroshi and tick which item they are talking about in each set above.

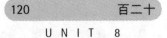

15

Survey at least five of your classmates to find out what colours they like or dislike in Japanese. Write the colour in the table.

なまえ	好きな　いろ	きらいな　いろ

16

Here is a basket of bingo balls. A colour is written on each ball. Put the colours which are nouns in one box and those which are adjectives in the other box.

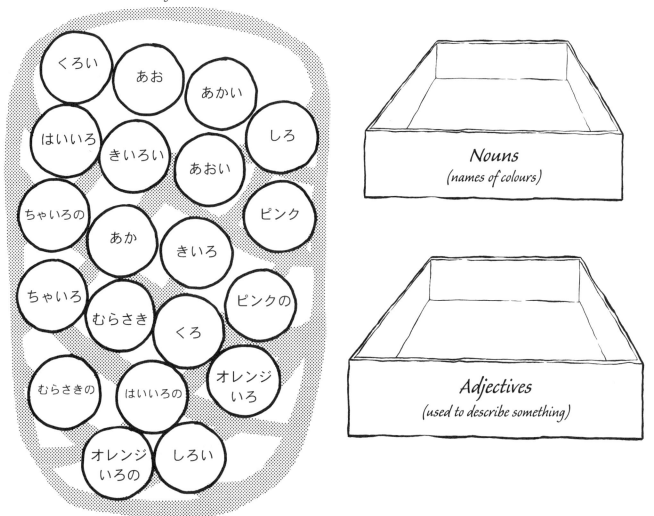

Nouns
(names of colours)

Adjectives
(used to describe something)

Using the key, number the sentence components.

Adjectives	1
Nouns	2
Verbs	3
Particles	4

a

くろ	が	好き	です。
2	4	1	3

b

ちゃいろの	りんご	は	おいしい	です。

c

しろい	車	を	うんてんしています。

d

しろ	が	きらい	です。

e

好きな	車	は	きいろい	ポルシェ	です。

Work out the calculations to find out which number has been assigned to each colour and then colour the picture appropriately. Before you begin colouring, check you have all the colours.

Number				Colour
九十七	ひく	九十四は ...		はいいろ
四十一	ひく	三十七は ...		くろ
千十一	ひく	千九は ...		きいろ
百八	わる	十八は ...		むらさき
百三十五	わる	二十七は ...		しろ
四千 たす	三百 ひく	四千二百九十二は ...		あお
百 かける	五百 わる	五万は...		あか
ルート		四十九は ...		みどり

ひく	minus	たす	plus
かける	times	わる	divided by
は...	equals	ルート	square root of

Here are some special car features. Write the English equivalents. Check your answers with a partner. Try reading them aloud.

a エアバッグ _____

b パワーシート _____

c オートエアコン _____

d アルミホイール _____

e ワイヤレスドアロック

_____

f リヤスポイラー _____

g パワーステアリング _____

h オートマチック _____

i ハンドル _____

j ワイパー _____

k フロントガラス _____

l バックミラー _____

m タイヤ _____

n バンパー _____

o ナビゲーションシステム

_____

p スピードメーター _____

q エンジン _____

r ドアミラー _____

s バックギア _____

t ターボ _____

20

If you owned these items, what colour would they be? Write a full sentence in Japanese as in the example.

a ペンは　<u>あおいです。</u>

b ねこ　_____

c ベッドカバー　_____

d ふてばこ　_____

e がっこうの　かばん　_____

f うちの　ドア　_____

g がっこうの　ジャンパー　_____

21

Make a handy phrasebook of at least twenty five Japanese phrases and their English equivalents. There may be lots of handy phrases from earlier units you sometimes can't remember. You might also like to include phrases from this unit. For example, いらっしゃいませ。

Welcome. (shop/restaurant)

You should remember that it is not a dictionary, but a collection of handy phrases and patterns. However, you might like to make a handy dictionary using this technique for future reference.

22

Find as many Japanese words and phrases as you can in the puzzle and make a list in your exercise book. Also write the English equivalent for each word. Characters may be used more than once. Words can be found horizontally from left to right and vertically from top to bottom. There are no diagonal words!

The word search can also be used as a competition. Your teacher might give you a time limit of 10 minutes. Each character in a word and the English equivalent are worth one point each. Who will get the most points? You can also do this task in pairs and add the totals. You will need to check the same word has not been used twice!

す	み	ま	せ	ん	だ	安	い	小	さ	い	か	ん	ぱ	い	フ	テ	レ	ビ	雪
う	べ	あ	れ	は	い	ス	テ	レ	オ	く	来	あ	見	オ	レ	ン	ジ	い	ろ
が	ん	大	き	い	じ	見	す	秋	左	ら	月	か	せ	右	｜	百	五	十	円
く	り	あ	お	い	ょ	ま	し	だ	め	で	す	く	ま	ど	ズ	来	ま	す	行
あ	な	た	は	ろ	う	し	そ	う	で	す	春	な	す	山	ブ	ま	買	ブ	け
ホ	む	ら	さ	き	ぶ	た	マ	ツ	ダ	か	本	い	月	見	ッ	せ	い	ル	ま
ン	さ	む	ら	い	う	ん	て	ん	し	ま	す	で	ん	わ	ク	ん	ま	ン	す
ダ	あ	し	高	い	で	き	い	て	い	ま	す	す	夏	何	ク	で	せ	ブ	三
ど	う	ぞ	き	い	ろ	い	で	り	ん	ご	お	つ	り	し	｜	し	ん	ル	万
き	ら	い	な	冬	大	雨	す	買	い	も	の	二	時	ろ	ペ	た	ペ	ン	円

おべんとう クイズ

1 Circle the correct answer.

a You would say おそくなって　すみません
when you are:
- going to sleep.
- leaving home.
- running late.
- interrupting a conversation.

b You would say きを　つけてください when
you want someone to:
- talk to you.
- telephone you.
- turn on the light.
- take care.

c When the customer says これを　ください
s/he means:
- s/he will take the bag.
- s/he will take this bag.
- s/he will take this one.
- s/he will take that one over there.

2 Match the Japanese with its English equivalent. Write
the letter beside the Japanese word or phrase.

フレーズブック	a small
あかい	b red
大きい	c purple
エアコン	d No, you may not.
見に　行きました	e phrasebook
小さい	f I'm listening.
きいています	g big
むらさき	h I went to see it.
高い	i brown
あけてもいいですか	j air conditioner
ちゃいろ	k May I open it?
だめです	l expensive/tall

3 Circle the odd one out.

a ABSブレーキ　ブルンブルン
シートベルト　　エアバッグ

b くろい　みどり　あおい　しろい

c かっこいい　おつり　しょうひぜい
五百円

4 Number the statements in the correct order in the
first column. Then write **S** (salesperson) or
C (customer) depending on who would say the
phrase.

(1) いらっしゃいませ。	S
( ) フレーズブックが　ありますか。	
( ) いくらですか。	
( ) 三百十五円です。	
( ) すみません、	
( ) 五円の　おつりです。	
( ) ええ、ありますよ。はい、どうぞ。	
( ) どうも　ありがとうございました。	
( ) じゃ、これを　ください。	

5 Complete the table.

I do	I am doing	May I?
よみます	よんでいます	よんでも いいですか
ききます		
たべます		
します		

6 Write a sentence in Japanese to describe what each
person is doing.

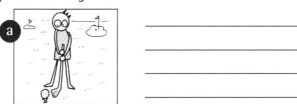

_____

_____

_____

_____

百二十五　　　　125

U N I T　8

b _____
_____
_____

c _____
_____
_____

7 Complete the following sentences using
これは, それは or あれは, as appropriate.

a 何ですか。

_____ ぼくの　すうがくの　本です。

b 何ですか。

_____ 大きい　くもです。

8 How would you answer if your younger brother or
sister asked you the following questions?

a へやに　はいっても　いいですか。

_____

b 大好きな　まんがを　よんでも
いいですか。

_____

c チョコレートを　ぜんぶ　たべても
いいですか。

_____

d テレビを　見ても　いいですか。

_____

9 How would you ask someone:

a if you may drive?

_____

b if you may listen to the radio?

_____

c if you may buy a Japanese phrasebook?

_____

d if you may go surfing tomorrow?

_____

10 Answer the questions using the clues given.

a オレンジいろですか。

はい、_____

b きいろいですか。

いいえ、_____

c ピンクですか。

いいえ、_____

d むらさきの　車ですか。

いいえ、_____

e はいいろの　電車は　おそいですね。

ええ、_____

f しろい　ねこは　かわいいですよ。

いいえ、_____

11 Answer the following questions truthfully in
Japanese in a full sentence.

a あかが　大好きですか。

_____

b あなたの　ペンは　みどりですか。

_____

c あなたの　うちは　きいろいですか。

_____

d しろい　車が　好きですか。

_____

unit 1

1

Using the pictures, complete the katakana words.

a ＿ ― ス ＿ ＿ リ ＿

b ＿ ＿ ＿ カ

c バ ＿ ＿ ッ ＿ ＿ ― ル

d ＿ イ ＿ ＿ ＿ ― ＿

2

Write the kanji for the following words. Then think about the English meaning.

a 　きん　よう　び　　　　　やす
　□ 曜 □ は 　□ みです。

b 　ろく　がつ　じゅう　ご　にち　　　　　に　ほん
　□ □ □ □ □ に 　□ □ に 　いきます。

c ともだちと 　□ □ で 　テレビを 　みます。
　　　　　　　　ふ　たり

1

Practise the kanji.

| | | Handwritten character | Printed character |

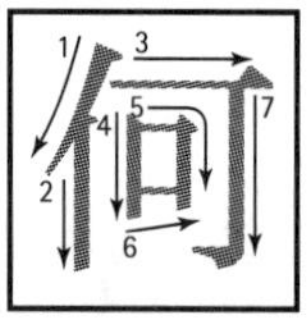

何　　何　　何

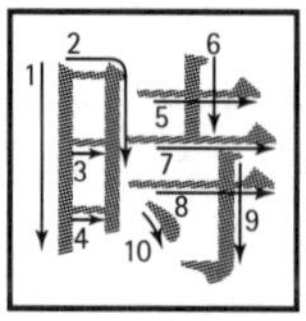

時　　時　　時

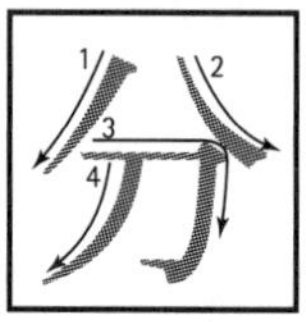

分　　分　　分

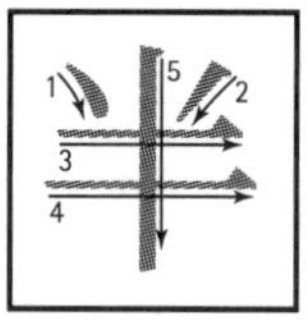

半　　半　　半

2

Read the following sentences and write the ふりがな above each かんじ. Then give the English meaning.

a 一、二、三、四、五、六、七...

one, two, three, four, five, six, seven...

b 日曜日は　休みです。

c かぞくは　□□何 人ですか。

___

d □□□九時半に　がっこうに　いきました。

___

Write the かんじ in the squares using the ふりがな as a guide. Then work out the English meaning.

a いま　<ruby>なん<rt></rt></ruby><ruby>じ<rt></rt></ruby>□□ですか。

b <ruby>はち<rt></rt></ruby><ruby>じ<rt></rt></ruby><ruby>ご<rt></rt></ruby><ruby>ふん<rt></rt></ruby>□□□□に　いきました。

c きょうは　<ruby>すい<rt></rt></ruby><ruby>よう<rt></rt></ruby><ruby>び<rt></rt></ruby>□□□ですね。

d ともだちが　<ruby>さん<rt></rt></ruby><ruby>じゅう<rt></rt></ruby><ruby>ろく<rt></rt></ruby><ruby>にん<rt></rt></ruby>□□□□です。

e たんじょう<ruby>び<rt></rt></ruby>□は　<ruby>く<rt></rt></ruby><ruby>がつ<rt></rt></ruby><ruby>ようか<rt></rt></ruby>□□□□です。

Join the following words in the correct order for each group. Use a different colour for each line.

a Days of the week: Monday - Saturday

b Days of the month: 1st - 31st

c Months of the year: January - December

d Half hours: 1 o'clock - 12.30

二十日	一日	七日	九月
三月	八時半	四月	六時
十一時半	十四日	四日	日曜日
三時半	二十六日	二時半	二十五日
火曜日	十九日	二十九日	三日
十六日	二月	金曜日	一月
八時	八月	五時半	十三日
五日	二十七日	二十一日	三時
五時	二日	十二時	十二月
二十八日	二時	十五日	水曜日
十時半	六日	二十四日	十時
月曜日	七月	四時	十八日
十月	九日	十二日	五月
七時半	一時半	七時	三十日
二十三日	六時半	一時	八日
十日	木曜日	九時	二十二日
十二時半	十一時	三十一日	十七日
九時半	土曜日	六月	四時半
	十一日	十一月	

1

かんじを　れんしゅうしてください。

2

よんでください。ふりがなを　かいてください。えいごの　いみも　かいてください。

a 三時五分前です。

---

b テーブルの　上に　あります。

---

c ベッドの　下に　しろが　います。

3

ふりがなを よんでください。かんじを かいてください。えいごの いみは 何ですか。

a つくえの □(した)に □(なに)が ありますか。

b はこの □(なか)に しゃしんが あります

c うちの □(まえ)に にんじゃが います。

d □(ほん)の□(うえ)に ペンが あります。

たからさがし (Treasure hunt)

Follow the ヒント(hints) to find the characters which will lead you to the たからもの (treasure)!

たからものは　どこに　ありますか

一　はこの　中に　あります。

二　本の　上に　あります。

三　テーブルの　下に　あります。

四　ベッドの　上に　あります。

五　本だなの　上に　あります。

六　アルバムの　中に　あります。

七　つくえの　前に　あります。

八　ぬいぐるみの　上に　あります。

九　本だなの　中に　あります。

十　ＣＤプレーヤーの　前に　あります。

十一　つくえの　上に　あります。

十二　えの　下に　あります。

十三　テレビの　上に　あります。

十四　いぬの　前に　あります。

十五　ペンの　下に　あります。

十六　ふでばこの　中に　あります。

1

かんじを　れんしゅうしてください。

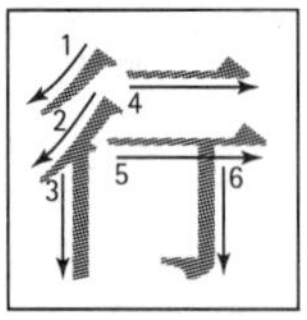 行	行							行	行
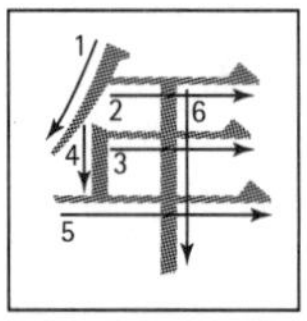 年	年							年	年
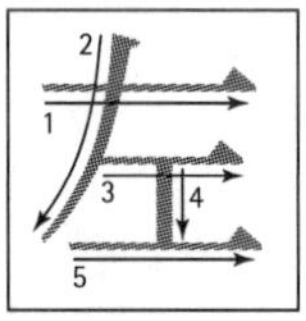 左	左							左	左
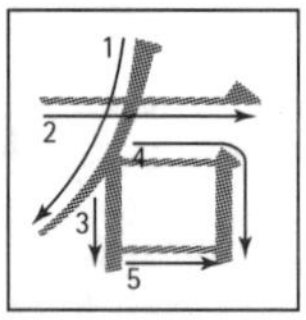 右	右							右	右

2

よんでください。ふりがなと　えいごの　いみを　かいてください。

a テレビの　左です。

_____

b わたしは　八年せいです。

_____

c 何時に　まちに　行きますか。

_____

□□□
d 四時半に おしろに 行きませんか。

□
e ペンは はこの 中に あります。

□□
f おかあさんの 右に おねえさんが
います。

ふりがなを よんでください。かんじを かいてください。えいごで いみは 何ですか。

a いり ぐち
□□からです。

b なん じ い
□□に □きましょうか。

c としょかんは えきの みぎ
□です。

d こうえんは ぎんこうの ひだり
□です。

かんじさがし

Colour the characters according to the number of strokes to find the hidden kanji.

三	前	分	行	金
月	ゴ	中	六	ネ
ど	何	五	時	木
ほ	火	ぱ	水	た
九	上	ふ	四	二
一	年	日	下	半
十	休	ビ	七	土

1 stroke grey   6 strokes blue
2 strokes purple   7 strokes pink
3 strokes green   8 strokes brown
4 strokes yellow   9 strokes orange
5 strokes red   10 strokes black

一, 二, 三, 四 …

5

The six monkeys are trying to hit Godzilla but not all of them strike a hit! Find out who does by following the kanji directions. For example, you must go left from a 左 square. Start at 入口.

やった!

出口

入口

くみ　　えみ　　ひろ　　ゆき　　とし　　まり

だれですか。

_____ です。

1

かんじを　れんしゅうしてください。

								春	春
夏								夏	夏
秋								秋	秋
冬								冬	冬

2

よんでください。ふりがなを　かいてください。えいごで　いみは　何ですか。

ⓐ 冬と　春が　すきです。

ⓑ 夏 休みに　アメリカに　行きます。

ⓒ 十 三 年ぐらい　すんでいます。

ⓓ 秋は 九月から 十一月までです。

ⓔ きょ年の 三月に 日本に きました

かんじを かいてください。えいごで いみは 何ですか。

ⓐ □□に □□に かえります。
（に がつ）（に ほん）

ⓑ □□みに □を しましたか。
（はる やす）（なに）

ⓒ なぜ □が すきですか。
（なつ）

ⓓ □まつりで やきいもを たべます。
（あき）

ⓔ □に いっしょに スキーを
しませんか。
（ふゆ）

You have learnt sixteen new kanji in *Obentoo 2*. Here is a puzzle which focuses on these sixteen kanji. Each kanji is made up of parts. From the chart, use the parts you need to make the sixteen kanji. Think about the correct stroke order as you make the kanji. Each part is only used once.

Cross off or highlight the parts as you use them and write the completed kanji in the squares.

Kanji parts

イ	彳	l	日	二	土	゛	ト
人	ト	工	テ	丁	刀	゛	ニ
日	口	ロ	ロ	リ	二	ナ	夂
⺊	八	月	一	寸	一	禾	l
夂	⊥	ナ	一	目	亠	l	火

Completed kanji

百三十九   139

1

かんじを　れんしゅうしてください。

女	女							女	女
男	男							男	男
子	子							子	子
山	山							山	山
雨	雨							雨	雨
雪	雪							雪	雪
電	電							電	電

電車	電	車						電車
電気	電	気						電気
天気	天	気						天気

よんでください。ふりがなを　かいてください。えいごの　いみは　何ですか。

a 電気を　けしてください。

b 雪子さんは　日本人です。

c いやな　天気です。雨です。

d あの　女の　人は　だれですか。

e きのう　電車で　山に　行きました。

f トムくんは　かわいい　男の　子です。

ふりがなを　よんでください。かんじを　かいてください。えいごの　いみは　何ですか。

a おんな
□の ひと□が なん□にん□いますか。

b おとこ□の こ□は テーブルの した□に います

c ピアノは でん□き□スタンドの みぎ□です

d わるい てん□き□です。 ゆき□です。

e ふゆ□やす□みに でん□しゃ□で ほっかいどうに い□きたいです。

Develop your own collage using at least twelve of the kanji you know. Cut pictures from magazines or newspapers or you can draw the items which you then label in kanji. Refer to the list of kanji at the back of your Student Book.

女の子

1

かんじを　れんしゅうしてください。

| 百 | | | | | | 百 | 百 |

 | 千 | | | | | | 千 | 千 |

 | 万 | | | | | | 万 | 万 |

 | 円 | | | | | | 円 | 円 |

2

よんでください。ふりがなを　かいてください。えいごの　いみは　何ですか。

ⓐ いくらですか。四百円 です。

ⓑ あのくつは　一万三千円です。

ⓒ この電気スタンドは　いくらですか。

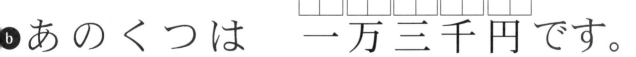

d 天ぷらを 九本 くださ い。

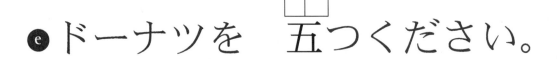

e ドーナツを 五つください。

3

ふりがなを　よんでください。かんじを　かいてください。えいごの　いみは　何ですか。

a <ruby>□<rt>なん</rt></ruby><ruby>□<rt>ぼん</rt></ruby>ですか。

b <ruby>□<rt>てん</rt></ruby>ぷらは　<ruby>□<rt>せん</rt></ruby><ruby>□<rt>はち</rt></ruby><ruby>□<rt>じゅう</rt></ruby><ruby>□<rt>えん</rt></ruby>です。

c <ruby>□<rt>に</rt></ruby><ruby>□<rt>せん</rt></ruby><ruby>□<rt>ねん</rt></ruby><ruby>□<rt>ご</rt></ruby><ruby>□<rt>がつ</rt></ruby><ruby>□<rt>さん</rt></ruby><ruby>□<rt>じゅう</rt></ruby><ruby>□<rt>いち</rt></ruby><ruby>□<rt>にち</rt></ruby>です。

d <ruby>□<rt>でん</rt></ruby><ruby>□<rt>しゃ</rt></ruby>の　きっぷは　<ruby>□<rt>さん</rt></ruby><ruby>□<rt>びゃく</rt></ruby><ruby>□<rt>なな</rt></ruby><ruby>□<rt>じゅう</rt></ruby><ruby>□<rt>えん</rt></ruby>です

e このステレオは　<ruby>□<rt>ろっ</rt></ruby><ruby>□<rt>ぴゃく</rt></ruby><ruby>□<rt>ご</rt></ruby><ruby>□<rt>じゅう</rt></ruby>ドルです

f こうべの　じんこうは　<ruby>□<rt>に</rt></ruby><ruby>□<rt>ひゃく</rt></ruby><ruby>□<rt>まん</rt></ruby><ruby>□<rt>にん</rt></ruby>です

Search for all the prices you can find and then write them out in kanji below. How much would it cost if you bought everything?

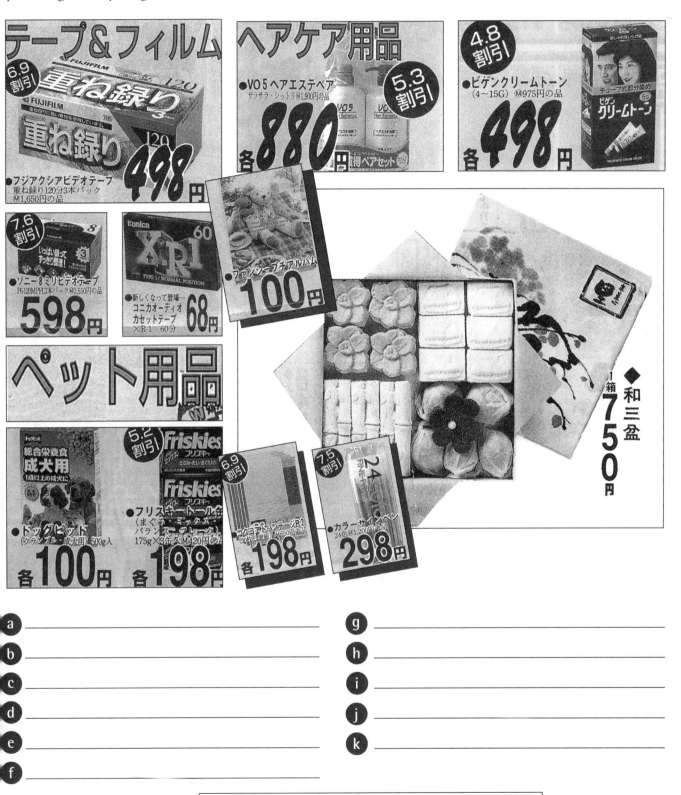

a	_____	g	_____
b	_____	h	_____
c	_____	i	_____
d	_____	j	_____
e	_____	k	_____
f	_____		

The total cost is: _____

1

かんじを　れんしゅうしてください。

	買							買	買
見	見							見	見
小	小							小	小
大	大							大	大
車	車							車	車
安	安							安	安
高	高							高	高
好	好							好	好

You, funny looking thing ....

2

よんでください。ふりがなを　かいてください。えいごの　いみも　かいてください。

a あの車は　高かったです。

b 小さい　じしょは　安いです。

c 大きい　ジュースを　買いました。

d いちばん　好きな　きせつは　秋です。

e テレビで　天気よほうを　見ました。

f あの女の　子は　何年せいですか。

3

ふりがなを よんでください。かんじを かいてください。えいごの いみは 何ですか。

ⓐ あしたの 　てんき　□□は 　ゆき□ です。

ⓑ 　に ほん□□の 　はる□が 　す□きです。

ⓒ な□は 　たか やま あき こ□□□□です。

ⓓ 　おお□きい 　でん しゃ□□で 　い□きました。

ⓔ 　ちい□さい 　くるま□を 　み□せてください。

ⓕ 　たか□い 　ほん□を 　か□いませんか。

ⓖ 　さん ねん はん□□□ぐらい 　やす□い アパートに

すんでいました。

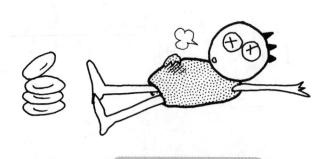

4

Storyteller's maze game

Start in the top row and work your way to the bottom of the maze square by square by making sentences using the kanji in the squares you move to. Write your sentences down. For each kanji you use, you gain the points indicated at the top of the square. The object is to win the most points in your class. Colour code each square as you win it. **You can only move diagonally down the squares.** You cannot move backwards and a square can only be used once.

四 車	五 電車	五 女の子	五 行きます	四 休み	四 日本ご	四 山	四 上	四 日本
五 見ます	五 小さい	五 天気	五 金曜日	五 雨	六 電気スタンド	四 夏	三 円	五 六時半
四 九	五 五時	六 大好きな	六 七月四日	四 下	五 十分	五 中山学園	ご 左	四 夏休み
五 水曜日	五 買います	五 右	四 冬	五 女の子	五 一万	四 五十円	五 男の子	七 行って
六 らい月	六 前	五 大きい	四 中	三 冬休み	六 三年ぐらい	三 春	五 大きらいな	五 買いもの
五 小さいいぬ	五 高い	五 男の人	三 秋	四 行きません	三 雪	四 見ました	三 土曜日	五 安い
五 安かった	四 五千	五 好きな	十 雪女	七 買って	八 高くない	三 百	七 はな見	七 十時まで
六 二年半	八 子ども	十 夏子	四 本だな	七 小さかった	五 何百	六 電わ	四 行きません	六 火曜日から
六 な前	十二 忍者	十 本しゅう	十 まい日	八 秋休み	五 九しゅう	十 天ぷら	十 八人	七 四本

Sentences

a _____   f _____

b _____   g _____

c _____   h _____

d _____   i _____

e _____   Score: _____

Japanese-English word lists

Unit 1

あいます	meet *(verb)*
あたらしい	new
あるいて	on foot
いきます	go *(verb)*
いってきます	see you later *(greeting for leaving home)*
いってらっしゃい	see you when you get back *(greeting when someone is leaving home)*
いつまでも	forever
いろいろありがとう	thank you for everything
うた	song
うたいます	sing *(verb)*
えいがかん	movie theatre
えき	station
おくれてすみません	I'm sorry I'm late
かいます	buy *(verb)*
かいもの	shopping
かきます	write *(verb)*
カラオケボックス	karaoke box
ききます	listen *(verb)*
きます	come *(verb)*
きをつけて！	take care!
くま	bear
ゲームセンター	game centre
げんきでね	take care of yourself
こうえん	park
ごご	pm
ごぜん	am
ことば	word
ごにん、五人	five people
さびしい	I feel lonely/I miss him/her
じ、時	o'clock
しつれいします	excuse me
します	do *(verb)*
ジム	gym
じゃ	well then
じゃあね！	see you!
じょうず（な）	good at it
しんかんせん	bullet train
スクールホール	school hall
すもう	sumo wrestling
だいがく	university
たいへん！	oh, no!
たのしみ	looking forward to it
たべます	eat *(verb)*
ちかてつ	subway
てがみかいてね!	write me a letter!
テスト	test
デパート	department store
でも	but

でんわしてね！	ring me!
どうも	thanks (short for どうも ありがとう)
としょかん	library
ともだちの ままで いましょう	let's stay friends
ニュース	news
ぬいぐるみ	soft toy
のみます	drink *(verb)*
のります	ride *(verb)*
パーティー	party
ハイキング	hiking
バイバイ！	bye bye!
はずかしい	embarrassing
はん、半	half past
ひこうき	aeroplane
ひっこし（を します）	move house *(verb)*
ひま	free/nothing to do
プール	pool
ふーん	hmmm...
ふね	ship
フランスご	French language
へ	Dear *(used in letters)*
へた（な）	bad at
べんきょうします	study *(verb)*
ポップコーン	popcorn
また	again
またきてね！	come again!
まち	town/city
みなさんに よろしく	say hello to everyone
みます	see/look/watch *(verb)*
もうすぐ	very soon
やきそば	fried noodles
やきとり	grilled chicken on skewers
よみます	read *(verb)*
より	from *(used in letters or memos)*
ロックバンド	rock band
わすれないで！	don't forget me!

_____ _____

_____ _____

_____ _____

_____ _____

_____ _____

Unit 2

アイススケート	ice-skating
あそびます	play/muck about *(verb)*
あつい	hot
あのー、しつれいですが	umm... excuse me but...
あのね、きいてよ	hey, listen

あら	oh	らいねん	next year
ありました	there was	レッスン	lesson
いいですね	that would be great	わー！	wow!
いいなあ	gee, that's great		
イーメール	email		
いそがしい	busy		
いつも	always		
いま	now		
うんうん	yeah, yeah		
ええ	yeah		
おじさん	uncle		
おしらせします	I am informing you	**Unit 3**	
おねがいします	please do me a favour	あそびに きてください	please come to visit
おばさん	aunt	あたらしい	new
ガールフレンド	girlfriend	アテネ	Athens
かえります	return (verb)	アパート	apartment
カンガルー	kangaroo	あります	there is/are, exist, have (non living things)
きょねん	last year		
げんき	well/healthy	アルバム	album
ことし	this year	いす	chair
こんげつ	this month	います	there is/are, exist, have (living things)
こんしゅう	this week		
さなえですが、たかこさん おねがいします	This is Sanae, can I speak to Takako please?	いまのうち	current house
		うえ、上	on top/above
さむい	cold	うしろ	behind
しゃしん	photo	かわいい	cute
しゃしんをとります	take photos	ギリシャ	Greece
せんげつ	last month	クリスマスツリー	Christmas tree
せんしゅう	last week	ゴジラ	Godzilla
そうかなあ	I wonder	コンピューター	computer
そうそう	yes it is	さっぽろ	Sapporo
そうなの？	is that right?	さむい	cold
それから、どうしたの？	what happened after that?	シーディー、CD	CD
たかい	expensive/high	シーディープレーヤー、 CDプレーヤー	CD player
たくさん	a lot		
チェス	chess	じしょ	dictionary
でかけます	go out (verb)	しずか（な）	quiet
でもさ…	but hey…	した、下	under, below
どうぶつえん	zoo	じてんしゃ	bicycle
とても	very	しゃしん	photograph
とります	take (verb)	すてき（な）	nice/lovely
なあんだ	is that all?	そと	outside
なるほど	I see	だいすき（な）	love/fantastic
ねます	sleep (verb)	ちいさい	small
はい、なんでしょう？	yes, what is it?	つくえ	desk
ひとりで、一人で	alone/by oneself	テーブル	table
ひまなとき	free time	てがみ	letter
ふん、ぷん、分	… minute(s)	～でしょう	don't you think?/probably
ふんまえ、分前	… minutes to	テレビ	television
へえー？	Whaat? Is that true?	でんきスタンド	desk lamp
へえ、じゃあ	oh, well then …	～と～	and
ボート	boat	トイレ	toilet
ほんと？	really?	とけい	watch/clock
みたいなあ	I'd like to see it.	どこ	where?
もしもし	hello (telephone)	どんな	what kind of?
やすい	cheap	なか、中	inside/middle
よかった	it was good	にわ	garden/yard
ヨット	yacht	はがき	post card
らいげつ	next month	はこ	box
らいしゅう	next week		

ヒーター	heater
ひっこしします	move house *(verb)*
ひろい	spacious/wide
ふでばこ	pencil case
ベッド	bed
へや	room
べんきょう	study
べんり（な）	handy/convenient
ほら！	hey, look!
ほんだな、本だな	bookshelf
まえ、前	before/in front/ago
またあいたいです	I want to see you again
まち	town/city
もう、うるさい！	that's enough/shut up!
〜や、〜や、など	and, and, etc
よこ	next to/beside

―――――――――
―――――――――
―――――――――
―――――――――

Unit 4

あおもり	Aomori
あたらしい	new
あたらしくない	not new
アデレード	Adelaide
ありがとう	thank you
ありがとうございました	thank you
あんまり	not really
いきましょう、行きましょう	let's go
いきましょうか、行きましょうか	shall we go?
いつまで	until when?
いつから	from when?
インターネット	internet
ええー？	oh? *(when hesitating)*
おおきくない	not big
おおさか	Osaka
おかし	sweets
おかしい	funny
おかしくない	not funny
おしろ	castle
おそい	slow
おそくない	not slow
おなじ	the same
おもい	heavy
おもくない	not heavy
カーニバル	carnival
かがく	science
かたな	Japanese warrior's sword
かもく	subject
〜から	from/because
カンティーン	canteen
きたない	dirty
きたなくない	not dirty
きっぷ	ticket

きれいじゃない	not nice/not clean/not pretty
クラス	class
けしき	scenery
こうべえき	Kobe station
ここです	it's here
コンサート	concert
さむらい	medieval Japanese warrior
しずかじゃない	not quiet
シドニー	Sydney
ジャカルタ	Jakarta
ジャズショー	jazz show
しゅくだい	homework
じょうず（な）	good at/skillful
じょうずじゃない	not good at/not skillful
スーパー	supermarket
すうがく	mathematics
すきじゃない	don't like
すてき（な）	nice/lovely
すてきじゃない	not nice/not lovely
スニーカー	sneakers
スポーツデー	sports day
すんでいます	live
セール	sale
ぜんぜん	not at all/never
たいいく	physical education
だいじょうぶ（な）	all right/safe, sound/certain
だいじょうぶじゃない	not all right/not safe, not sound/not certain
だいじょうぶです	that's all right/that's fine
だいすきじゃない	don't like very much
たかい	expensive/high
たかくない	not expensive/not high
たてもの	building
タワー	tower
ちいさくない	not small
ちかい	near *(adjective)*
ちかく	near *(adverb)*
ちかくない	not near
ちょっと	a bit
ちり	geography
ディズニーランド	Disneyland
でぐち、出口	exit
デパート	department store
でました	left/went out
でんとうてき（な）	traditional
でんとうてきじゃない	not traditional
どうもありがとうございます	thank you very much
とおい	far
とおくない	not far
どこから	where from?
どこまで	where to?
とても	very
どのぐらい	how long?
トム・クルーズ	Tom Cruise
トラック	truck
なんじから、何時から	what time from?
なんじまで、何時まで	what time until?
はやい	fast/quick
はやく！	hurry up!
はやくない	not fast/not quick

はれ	sunny/fine weather
パンフレット	pamphlet
ひだり、左	left
ひまです	free/nothing to do
ひめじ	Himeji
ひめじじょう	Himeji Castle
ひろくない	not spacious/not wide
ひろしま	Hiroshima
ふくおか	Fukuoka
ブリスベン	Brisbane
ヘリコプター	helicopter
べんりじゃない	not handy/not convenient
まだ	yet
まつやま	Matsuyama
〜まで	to/until
みぎ、右	right
みせ	shop
むかし	long ago
むずかしい	difficult
むずかしくない	not difficult
もってください	please hold it
ゆうびんきょく	post office
ゆうめい（な）	famous
ゆうめいじゃない	not famous
れきし	history

_____   _____
_____   _____
_____   _____
_____   _____

Unit 5

あき、秋	autumn
あきまつり、秋まつり	autumn festival
あけましておめでとう	Happy New Year!
ございます	
アストロボーイ	Astroboy
あそび	play (noun)
アトラクション	attraction
あの	that (over there)
アルゼンチン	Argentina
いちにちめ、一日め	the first day
いちばん	the most...
いつ	when?
いろいろなこと	various things
おせちりょうり	New Year food
おつきみ	moonviewing
おとしだま	money gift at New Year
おもち	rice cake
およぎ	swim (noun)
おんせんにはいります	go into a hot spring
かきごおり	shaved ice treat
かどまつ	New Year decoration
カメラ	camera
から	because
からだにいい	good for your body
かわいそうねえ	I feel sorry for him/her

きせつ	season
きもちがいい	feeling good
きれいにさきます	bloom prettily
こうよう	autumn colours
こくりつこうえん	National Park
ことしもよろしく	please be my friend this year too
おねがいします	
この	this
ごめんね	sorry
サーフィンをします	go surfing
サイクリングをします	go cycling
さくら	cherry blossom
さくらぜんせん	cherry blossom line
さる	monkey
さんぽ	a walk/a stroll
じゆう	freedom
しゅうがくりょこう	a school trip
しょくじつき	meals included
しんねんおめでとう	Happy New Year!
ございます	
すいじょうスキーをします	go water skiing
スーパー	supermarket
スノーボードをします	go snowboarding
すばらしい	fantastic
スペースワールド	Space World
その	that (near you)
タイタン	Titan
たのしみね！	I look forward to it!
つくります	make (verb)
つりにいきます/行きます	go fishing
つれませんでした	I couldn't catch it
どうぶつ	animal
どの	which one?
ドライブに	go for a drive
いきます/行きます	
ながい	long
なぜ	why?
なつ、夏	summer
にぎやかね	lively, isn't it?
ねんがじょう、年がじょう	New Year card
はいります	enter/go in (verb)
はな	flower
はなび	fireworks
はる、春	spring
はるかぜ	a spring wind
パンダ	panda
バンド	music band
ひと、人	person
ひなにんぎょう	Girls' Day dolls
ふゆ、冬	winter
フリーフォール	Free fall
ふるさと	hometown
ボートにのります	ride on a boat
ポケモン	Pokemon
もらいます	receive (verb)
やきいも	roast sweet potato
やまのぼり	mountain climbing
ゆきだるま	snowman
ようしょく	Western food
よっかかん、四日かん	for four days

りょこうをします	go on a trip	たいふう	typhoon/cyclone
リラックスします	relax *(verb)*	たらたら	sweating
ろてんぶろ	outdoor bath	ちかく	neighbourhood/area
わしょく	Japanese food	ちほう	region
		つけます	to switch on (an appliance)
		ディスクマン	diskman
		できる	to be able to
		でしょう	might be
		てんき、天気	weather
		てんきよほう、天気よほう	weather report
		でんきをけします、電気を	switch off the light
		けします	

Unit 6

あさって	the day after tomorrow	テント	tent
あたたかい	warm	ところがあるふゆのひ、	but one winter day
あなたはまだこどもです	you are still a child	ところがある冬の日	
あのこやに行こう	let's go to that shack	なぜ	why?
アフリカ	Africa	なんど、何ど	how many degrees?
あめ、雨	rain	にている	to look like (someone)/resemble
あらし	storm	のち	later
あるゆきのよる、	one snowy night	はーっ	the sound of breathing out loud
ある雪のよる		バタン	the sound of a door closing
ウエイトトレーニング	weight training	パリ	Paris
ウォーミングアップを	warm up	ハリウッド	Hollywood
します		ビーチ	beach
うれしいなあ	I'm so happy	ひぇー	the sound of a terrified scream
エアコン	airconditioner	ひきます	play an instrument (piano) *(verb)*
エアロビクス	aerobics	（ピアノをひきます）	
えど	Tokyo *(old name)*	ビュービュー	the sound of strong winds
おげんきですか	how are you?		blowing
かさ	umbrella	ブッシュウォーキング	bushwalking
かぜがつよい	strong wind	ふぶき	blizzard
カチンカチン	the sound of ice forming	ブラジリア	Brasilia
きおん	temperature	ぶるぶる	shivering
ぎらぎら	pulsating heat from the sun	ぽかぽか	warmth
クーラー	air cooler	ぼつぼつ	the sound of rain beginning
くもり	cloudy	ミーティング	meeting
ケープタウン	Cape Town	むかしむかし	once upon a time
けします	switch off (an appliance)	むしあつい	humid
こんこん	the sound of heavy snow	もうすぐ	soon/immediately
こんな	this kind of	モスクワ	Moscow
こんや	this evening	ゆき、雪	snow
サーキットトレーニングを	do circuit training	ゆきおんなにそっくりだ、	she looks just like the
します		雪女にそっくりだ	Snow woman
ざあざあ	the sound of heavy rain	ゆきになる、雪になる	begin snowing
さいこうきおん	highest temperature	ラスベガス	Las Vegas
さいていきおん	lowest temperature	レナルド・ディカプリオ	Leonardo DiCaprio
さむざむ	chilly/draughty	ロスアンゼルス	Los Angeles
しとしと	the sound of sprinkling rain		
ジョギング	jogging		
すずしい	cool		
ストーブをつけます	switch on the heater		
せかいのてんき、	world weather		
せかいの天気			
せんしゅ	athlete		
せんぷうき	fan		
そのあと	after that		

Unit 7

そのかわり、わたしの	in return, don't tell anyone	あけられます	can open
ことはだれにもいわないで	about me	あけられません	can't open
		あじビル	Aji building

いくつ	how many?	つかえません	can't use
いくらですか	how much is it?	つくれます	can make
いけます、行けます	can go	つくれません	can't make
いけません、行けません	can't go	できます	can do
いす	chair	できません	can't do
いただきます	thanks before a meal	デザート	dessert
イタリア	Italy	てんぷら、天ぷら	tempura
いちまん、一万	ten thousand/10,000	どうぞ	here you are
いつつ、五つ	five (general items)	とうふステーキ	beancurd steak
いっぴんりょうり	a la carte dishes	ドーナツ	doughnut
いらっしゃいませ	can I help you?/welcome	とりてりやき	grilled skewered chicken with teriyaki sauce ·
えん、円	yen	とんかつ	crumbed pork cutlet
おなかいっぱい	I'm full	ななひゃくドル、七百ドル	seven hundred dollars/$700
おなかペコペコ	I'm starving	なにしますか、何にしますか	what will you have?
おはし	chopsticks		
かけます	can write	なべもの	hot pot dishes
かけません	can't write	なまの さかな	raw fish
かしこまりました	certainly	なんばい、何ばい	how many cups?
カップケーキ	cup cake	なんぼん、何本	how many bottles?
かな	I wonder	におい	smell/aroma
かばん	bag	～にします	to decide on
カリフォルニアロール	californian roll	のみもの	drinks
カレーうどん	soup noodles with curry sauce	のめます	can drink
かんじ	Chinese characters	のめません	can't drink
かんぱい	cheers	～はい	counter for liquids
ぎょうざ	Japanese style dim sims	はい、かしこまりました	yes, certainly
～をください	please ...	はな	nose
くち	mouth	はなします	speak (verb)
ゲップ	burping sound	バンジージャンプ	bungee jump
ごせん、五千	five thousand/5,000	ハンバーグ	hamburger
ごひゃく、五百	five hundred	ビール	beer
ごはい、五はい	five cups	ピザ	pizza
ごほん、五本	five bottles	ひとつ、一つ	one item
ごまん、五万	fifty thousand/50,000	ひゃく、百	(one) hundred
ごまんごせんごひゃくごじゅうご、五万五千五百五十五	fifty five thousand five hundred and fifty five/55,5555	ひゃくごじゅう、百五十	one hundred and fifty/150
		ピンポン	ping pong
		ほん、本	counter for long cylindrical items
こられます	can come		
こられません	can't come	フォーク	fork
コロッケ	croquette	ペン	pen
ゴルフ	golf	みず、水	water
コンピューターゲーム	computer game	みみ	ear
サイダー	cider	みられます	can see
さんぽ	a walk/stroll	みられません	can't see
しめられます	can shut	め	eye
しめられません	can't shut	もてます	can hold/can carry
しゃぶしゃぶ	meat cooked in broth with vegetables	もてません	can not hold/can not carry
		やきとり	grilled chicken on skewers
すきやき	sukiyaki	よせなべ	chowder
スプーン	spoon	よめます	can read
すわれます	can sit	よめません	can't read
すわれません	can't sit	りょうり	cooking/cuisine
せん、千	(one) thousand	りんご	apple
そのほかに	apart from that	ろっぴゃくえん、六百円	six hundred yen/600 yen
そば	buckwheat noodles	ワイン	wine
たべられます	can eat	わかめうどん	noodles with seaweed
たべられません	can't eat		
チョコレートパフェ	chocolate parfait		
つかえます	can use		

_____ _____
_____ _____
_____ _____
_____ _____

Unit 8

あお（い）	blue
あか（い）	red
あけてもいいです	you may open it
あけます	open (verb)
あそんでいます	playing (verb)
あれは	that one (over there)
あれも	that one too
いくじしょ	nursery
いってもいいです、 行ってもいいです	you may go
うんてんします	drive (verb)
うんてんしています	driving (verb)
うんてんしてもいいです	you may drive
エービーエスブレーキ、 ABSブレーキ	ABS brakes
エアバッグ	air bag
えきまえ、えき前	before the station
エスカレーター	escalator
おおきすぎます、 大きすぎます	too big
オートマチックの	automatic
おきます	get up
おそくなってすみません	sorry I'm late
おつり	change
およいでもいいです	you may swim
オレンジいろ（の）	orange
かいています	writing (verb)
かっこいい	cool/great
かっています、 買っています	buying (verb)
かってもいいです、 買ってもいいです	you may buy
きいています	listening (verb)
きいろ（い）	yellow
クーペ	coupe
くも	cloud
くろ（い）	black
こちらへ	this way
こみ	gross/includes
これは	this one
これをください	this one please
さわっています	touching (verb)
さわってもいいです	you may touch
さんかい、三かい	second floor
シートベルト	seat belt
じしょ	dictionary
しています	doing (verb)
してもいいです	you may do
ジャンパー	jumper
しょうひぜい	consumption tax

しろ（い）	white
スカート	skirt
すわっています	sitting (verb)
すわってもいいです	you may sit
すわります	sit (verb)
セーター	sweater
ソファ	sofa
それは	that one
だいきらい（な）、 大きらい（な）	hate
ダブルベッド	double bed
たべています	eating (verb)
たべてもいいです	you may eat
たんご	vocabulary/word
ちゃいろ（の）	brown
ついています	attached (verb)
つかってもいいです	you may use
つくっています	making (verb)
でんわしてもいいです、 電わしてもいいです	you may telephone
どういたしまして	you are welcome
どれ	which one?
ドレス	dress
のっています	riding (verb)
のってもいいです	you may ride
のんでもいいです	you may drink
はいいろ（の）	grey
はいってもいいです	you may enter
はしっています	running (verb)
ピンク（の）	pink
ふるい	old
ブルンブルン	brum brum (car sound)
フレーズブック	phrasebook
ベッドカバー	bed cover
べんきょうしています	studying (verb)
ホストファミリー	host family
ポルシェ	Porsche
ほんや、本や	bookshop
まちます	wait (verb)
マツダ	Mazda
見せます	show (verb)
ミツビシ	Mitsubishi
みています、見ています	looking/seeing/watching (verb)
みてもいいです、 見てもいいです	you may see
みどり（の）	green
むらさき（の）	purple
よんでいます	reading (verb)
よんでもいいです	you may read
りんご	apple
れんしゅうしています	practising (verb)
れんしゅうしてもいいです	you may practise

_____ _____
_____ _____
_____ _____
_____ _____
_____ _____